STECK-VAUGHN • TEACHER'S

WORKING *with* Numbers

LEVEL E

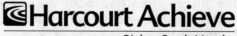
Meet your state standards with free blackline masters and links to other materials at
www.HarcourtAchieve.com/AchievementZone.
Click Steck-Vaughn Standards.

Harcourt Achieve
Rigby • Steck-Vaughn

www.HarcourtAchieve.com
1.800.531.5015

Contents

Acknowledgments

Cover Photo: © Chris Tomaidis/Stone

ISBN 0-7398-9166-9

© 2004 Harcourt Achieve Inc.

About the Program

Working with Numbers provides practice in key mathematics skills and strategies as outlined in the National Council of Teachers of Mathematics *Standards 2000*. The program incorporates the goals and concepts of The Standards including mastery of computational skills, the ability to choose and use appropriate problem-solving strategies, thinking and reasoning, and understanding the language of mathematics. Students using the program will also find ample applications of key mathematics strands such as algebra and geometry.

Student Book Features

Clear Presentation of Concepts

The mathematical skills lessons consist of one or two pages. A clear and precise explanation of the algorithm being taught begins each lesson. In the practice exercises that follow, initial problems are solved in a manner that models the presentation of the algorithm. This provides students with an immediate reference when deciding how to solve the computation problems. Each instructional lesson focuses on a single skill or strategy. Follow-up lessons expand concepts and include mixed practice and problem-solving applications.

The Language of Mathematics

Students are introduced to the language of mathematics in the context of instructional information and sample problems. Lessons provide key vocabulary in mathematics and the different synonyms that may be used. Examples and hints to the students support the meaning of mathematical terms. Practice is provided that applies the use of different terms, different ways to ask similar questions, and various problem formats.

Attention to Practice

Every skill lesson includes *Practice* exercises that provide the drill and practice necessary for positive reinforcement of the algorithm. Sample problems are provided to ensure that students understand the concepts before completing the computations on their own. Sufficient work space has been provided to allow students to work on the page itself.

Several times in each unit, *Mixed Practice* exercises are included on the second page of a two-page lesson. Constant reinforcement of previously taught skills ensures retention of those skills. The *Mixed Practice* exercises vary from lesson to lesson throughout the book to constantly reinforce skills that were taught in previous lessons.

Concepts are practiced and expanded in multiple follow-up lessons. Skill practice is broken into several stages of progression to allow students to master rudimentary skills before demonstrating higher levels of application. The progression from one lesson to the next allows students to slowly and methodically apply what they have learned to increasingly difficult algorithms.

Review and Assessment

Unit Review pages end each unit and provide exercises similar to those in the lessons. These include computational or mathematical content strand problems and a page of problem-solving strategy review. *Unit Reviews* may be used as end-of-unit tests.

Each student book ends with a comprehensive *Final Review*. Exercises that appear in the *Final Review* parallel those in the *Pretest* and in the *Mastery Test* found in this Teacher's Guide.

Problem Solving and Reasoning

Each unit includes two *Problem-Solving Strategy* lessons and two *Problem-Solving Applications* pages. The *Problem-Solving Strategy* pages provide activities that bridge the mastery of mathematical skills and the application of mathematics in solving real-life problems. These strategies provide the flexibility to encourage students to become better problem solvers. Strategies give students tools to experiment, discover, and explore a variety of ways to solve a given problem.

The four problem-solving steps—*Understand, Plan, Solve,* and *Look Back*—provide a logical process for solving problems. *Problem-Solving Applications* provide practice choosing strategies, using unit skills, and making sure answers make sense.

Teacher's Guide Features

The Teacher's Guide for each level includes an overview of the program, scope and sequence charts for mathematics skills and problem-solving strategies, teaching strategies and activities for each unit, a *Pretest,* a *Mastery Test,* and tests for each unit. Answer keys for the student books and blackline masters are also included.

Teaching Strategies

Each Teacher's Guide provides suggestions for instruction in unit concepts. For each unit, key vocabulary, objectives, introductory activities, and developmental activities are provided. Emphasis is given to *The Language of Mathematics, Reinforcement Activities,* and *Problem-Solving Activities.*

Blackline Masters

Unit Tests, Pretests, and *Mastery Tests* are provided in standardized test format. The *Pretest* and *Mastery Test* are each four pages in length and parallel the *Final Review* in the corresponding student worktext.

Scope and Sequence Chart

The scope and sequence of skills is based on the National Council of Teachers of Mathematics *Standards 2000* and current mathematics basal programs. Skills and problem-solving strategies progress logically and developmentally.

Meet your state standards with free blackline masters and links to other materials at **www.HarcourtAchieve.com/AchievementZone**. Click **Steck-Vaughn Standards**.

Scope and Sequence

	Level A	Level B	Level C	Level D	Level E	Level F
Place Value and Number Sense						
Counting and Skip Counting	•	•	•	•		
Writing Numbers and Number Words	•	•	•	•	•	
Understanding Larger Numbers	•	•	•	•	•	•
Using Place-Value Charts	•	•	•	•		
Comparing and Ordering Numbers	•	•	•	•		
Addition						
Basic Facts	•	•	•	•		
Fact Families	•	•	•	•		
2-digit Addition without Regrouping			•	•	•	•
2-digit Addition with Regrouping			•	•	•	•
3 and More Digits without Regrouping		•	•	•	•	•
3 and More Digits with Regrouping			•	•	•	•
Subtraction						
Basic Facts	•	•	•	•		
Fact Families	•	•	•	•		
2-digit Subtraction without Regrouping		•	•	•	•	•
2-digit Subtraction with Regrouping		•	•	•	•	•
3 and More Digits without Regrouping		•	•	•	•	•
3 and More Digits with Regrouping			•	•	•	•
Multiplication						
Basic Facts			•	•		
Fact Families			•	•		
2-digit Multiplication without Regrouping			•	•	•	•
2-digit Multiplication with Regrouping			•	•	•	•
3 and More Digits without Regrouping					•	•
3 and More Digits with Regrouping					•	•
Division						
Basic Facts			•	•		
Fact Families			•	•		
2-digit Division without Regrouping				•	•	•
2-digit Division with Regrouping				•	•	•
3 and More Digits without Regrouping					•	•
3 and More Digits with Regrouping					•	•
Money						
Recognizing Coins and Values	•	•				
Counting Money	•	•				
Comparing Equivalent Amounts	•	•				
Making Change		•				
Computations Using Money		•	•		•	•

	Level A	Level B	Level C	Level D	Level E	Level F
Time						
Digital and Analog Clocks	•	•				
Telling Time—Hours	•	•				
Telling Time—Half Hours	•	•				
Telling Time—Minutes		•	•	•		
Elapsed Time			•	•		
Calendar				•		
Measurement						
Nonstandard Units	•					
Customary Units	•	•	•	•	•	•
Metric Units	•	•	•	•	•	•
Geometry						
Solid Figures	•	•				
Plane Figures	•	•				
Congruence	•	•				•
Symmetry	•	•				
Perimeter		•	•	•	•	•
Points, Lines, and Angles			•	•	•	•
Area			•	•	•	•
Volume						•
Fractions						
Parts of a Whole			•			
Parts of a Group			•			
Comparing and Ordering Fractions				•	•	•
Computations with Fractions				•	•	•
Decimals						
Decimals and Place Value					•	•
Comparing and Ordering Decimals					•	•
Computations with Decimals					•	•
Relating Decimals and Fractions					•	•
Algebra						
Properties of Whole Numbers	•	•	•	•		•
Number Sentences	•	•	•	•	•	•
Missing Addends	•	•	•	•	•	•
Missing Factors			•	•	•	•
Equivalent Expressions	•	•	•	•	•	•
Input / Output Tables			•	•	•	•
Formulas			•	•	•	•
Order of Operations	•	•	•	•	•	•
Variables					•	•

Problem-Solving Scope and Sequence

Problem-Solving Strategies

	Level A	Level B	Level C	Level D	Level E	Level F
Use a Picture or Make a Drawing	•	•	•	•	•	•
Find or Complete a Pattern	•	•	•	•	•	•
Use or Make a Graph or Table	•	•	•	•	•	•
Make a List			•	•		•
Choose an Operation	•	•	•	•	•	•
Write a Number Sentence	•	•	•	•	•	•
Use Estimation		•	•	•	•	•
Use Guess and Check	•	•	•	•	•	•
Solve Multi-Step Problems				•	•	•
Identify Extra Information			•	•	•	•
Work Backwards			•	•	•	•
Use a Formula				•	•	•
Use Logic	•	•	•	•	•	•
Make a Model	•	•	•	•	•	

Additional Problem-Solving Strategies Supported in the Teacher's Guide

	Level A	Level B	Level C	Level D	Level E	Level F
Communicating Mathematically						
Demonstrate Reasoning by Drawing	•	•	•	•	•	•
Demonstrate Reasoning by Writing	•	•	•	•	•	•
Demonstrate Reasoning by Talking	•	•	•	•	•	•
Use the Language of Mathematics	•	•	•	•	•	•
Making Connections						
Relate Different Mathematical Ideas	•	•	•	•	•	•
Make Cross-Curricular Connections	•	•	•	•	•	•
Use Everyday Experiences	•	•	•	•	•	•

Pretest

1. Write the value of the underlined digit in 2,8<u>7</u>5,694.

   Ⓐ 80,000   Ⓒ 800,000
   Ⓑ 8,000   Ⓓ 8,000,000

2. Write one million, four hundred twenty thousand, fifteen using digits.

   Ⓐ 142,015   Ⓒ 1,402,015
   Ⓑ 1,420,150   Ⓓ 1,420,015

3. Add.   4,569
            + 621

   Ⓐ 3,948   Ⓒ 5,180
   Ⓑ 5,190   Ⓓ 4,180

4. Add.   217
            654
           + 435

   Ⓐ 1,306   Ⓒ 1,296
   Ⓑ 1,206   Ⓓ 1,360

5. Subtract.   504
                − 153

   Ⓐ 451   Ⓒ 657
   Ⓑ 357   Ⓓ 351

6. Add.   25,364
           + 19,024

   Ⓐ 6,340   Ⓒ 34,388
   Ⓑ 44,388   Ⓓ 44,088

7. Subtract.   45,630
               − 8,971

   Ⓐ 54,601   Ⓒ 36,659
   Ⓑ 36,661   Ⓓ 47,769

8. Estimate.   517
               + 287

   Ⓐ 800   Ⓒ 700
   Ⓑ 600   Ⓓ 900

9. Estimate.   4,879
              − 614

   Ⓐ 4,200   Ⓒ 5,500
   Ⓑ 4,000   Ⓓ 4,300

10. Multiply.   85
              × 6

    Ⓐ 515   Ⓒ 91
    Ⓑ 480   Ⓓ 510

11. Multiply. $3 \times 678 =$ _____

    Ⓐ 914   Ⓒ 681
    Ⓑ 2,034   Ⓓ 2,014

12. Multiply.   74
              × 79

    Ⓐ 5,772   Ⓒ 5,698
    Ⓑ 5,476   Ⓓ 5,846

13. Multiply. $42 \times 607 =$ _____

    Ⓐ 25,884   Ⓒ 25,494
    Ⓑ 3,642   Ⓓ 649

14. Estimate.   89
              × 62

    Ⓐ 5,400   Ⓒ 5,600
    Ⓑ 4,800   Ⓓ 4,200

15. Multiply.   835
$$\times\ 109$$

  Ⓐ 8,350   Ⓒ 91,015

  Ⓑ 15,865   Ⓓ 944

16. Multiply. $25 \times 4,893 =$ _____

  Ⓐ 122,325   Ⓒ 34,251

  Ⓑ 111,225   Ⓓ 4,918

17. Divide. $985 \div 5 =$ _____

  Ⓐ 17 R3   Ⓒ 197

  Ⓑ 190 R5   Ⓓ 990

18. Divide. $7\overline{)362}$

  Ⓐ 50 R5   Ⓒ 50 R12

  Ⓑ 51 R5   Ⓓ 50 R2

19. Divide. $3\overline{)316}$

  Ⓐ 15 R1   Ⓒ 105 R1

  Ⓑ 150 R1   Ⓓ 10 R5

20. Divide. $40\overline{)6,240}$

  Ⓐ 1,560   Ⓒ 156

  Ⓑ 150 R24   Ⓓ 15 R24

21. Estimate. $6\overline{)475}$

  Ⓐ 80   Ⓒ 8

  Ⓑ 70   Ⓓ 7

22. Divide. $23\overline{)1,586}$

  Ⓐ 69   Ⓒ 69 R9

  Ⓑ 68   Ⓓ 68 R22

23. Write three tenths as a fraction.

  Ⓐ $\frac{1}{3}$ Ⓒ $\frac{3}{10}$

  Ⓑ $\frac{3}{1,000}$ Ⓓ $\frac{3}{100}$

24. Write an equivalent fraction for $\frac{4}{8}$.

  Ⓐ $\frac{1}{4}$ Ⓒ $\frac{1}{8}$

  Ⓑ $\frac{1}{2}$ Ⓓ $\frac{2}{6}$

25. Write $\frac{16}{5}$ as a mixed number.

  Ⓐ $3\frac{1}{5}$ Ⓒ $2\frac{1}{5}$

  Ⓑ $\frac{1}{5}$ Ⓓ $4\frac{1}{5}$

26. Write $2\frac{3}{4}$ as an improper fraction.

  Ⓐ $\frac{6}{4}$ Ⓒ $\frac{5}{4}$

  Ⓑ $\frac{8}{4}$ Ⓓ $\frac{11}{4}$

27. Add. Simplify. $\frac{3}{7} + \frac{2}{7} =$ _____

  Ⓐ $\frac{5}{7}$ Ⓒ $\frac{1}{7}$

  Ⓑ $\frac{5}{14}$ Ⓓ $\frac{6}{7}$

28. Subtract. Simplify. $\frac{5}{9} - \frac{4}{9} =$ _____

  Ⓐ $\frac{9}{9}$ Ⓒ $\frac{1}{9}$

  Ⓑ $\frac{20}{9}$ Ⓓ $\frac{4}{5}$

29. Subtract. Simplify. $4\frac{3}{4} - 1\frac{2}{4} =$ _____

  Ⓐ 3   Ⓒ $5\frac{5}{4}$

  Ⓑ $2\frac{1}{4}$ Ⓓ $3\frac{1}{4}$

30. Add. Simplify. $\frac{3}{5} + \frac{1}{3} =$ _____

  Ⓐ $\frac{4}{8}$ Ⓒ $\frac{1}{2}$

  Ⓑ $\frac{4}{5}$ Ⓓ $\frac{14}{15}$

Name _____

31. Subtract. Simplify. $\frac{5}{8} - \frac{1}{2} =$ _____

Ⓐ $\frac{6}{10}$ Ⓒ $\frac{1}{8}$

Ⓑ $\frac{2}{3}$ Ⓓ $\frac{4}{6}$

32. Add. Simplify. $1\frac{1}{2} + 2\frac{1}{4} =$ _____

Ⓐ $3\frac{2}{6}$ Ⓒ $3\frac{1}{3}$

Ⓑ $3\frac{3}{4}$ Ⓓ $\frac{3}{4}$

33. Add. Simplify. $3\frac{2}{5} + 1\frac{3}{4} =$ _____

Ⓐ $4\frac{5}{9}$ Ⓒ $3\frac{5}{9}$

Ⓑ $4\frac{3}{20}$ Ⓓ $5\frac{3}{20}$

34. Subtract. Simplify. $2\frac{2}{3} - 1\frac{1}{5} =$ _____

Ⓐ $1\frac{1}{5}$ Ⓒ $1\frac{7}{15}$

Ⓑ $1\frac{1}{3}$ Ⓓ $3\frac{1}{17}$

35. Subtract. Simplify. $6 - 3\frac{4}{5} =$ _____

Ⓐ $3\frac{4}{5}$ Ⓒ $3\frac{1}{5}$

Ⓑ $2\frac{1}{5}$ Ⓓ $9\frac{4}{5}$

36. Write the value of the underlined digit in 1.5$\underline{6}$7.

Ⓐ 6 tenths   Ⓒ 6 thousandths

Ⓑ 6 hundredths   Ⓓ 6 hundreds

37. Write sixty-five thousandths as a decimal.

Ⓐ 65   Ⓒ 6.5

Ⓑ 0.65   Ⓓ 0.065

38. Compare.   1.76 _____ 1.760
Write <, >, or =.

Ⓐ <   Ⓒ =

Ⓑ >   Ⓓ not here

39. Write 0.05 as a fraction.

Ⓐ $\frac{1}{5}$ Ⓒ $\frac{5}{10}$

Ⓑ $\frac{5}{1,000}$ Ⓓ $\frac{5}{100}$

40. Add. $\begin{array}{r} 6.48 \\ + 3.75 \\ \hline \end{array}$

Ⓐ 10.23   Ⓒ 1.023

Ⓑ 1.23   Ⓓ 102.3

41. Estimate by rounding to the nearest one. $\begin{array}{r} 14.6 \\ + 5.3 \\ \hline \end{array}$

Ⓐ 19   Ⓒ 20

Ⓑ 17   Ⓓ 18

42. Subtract. $\begin{array}{r} \$10.76 \\ - 5.99 \\ \hline \end{array}$

Ⓐ $5.77   Ⓒ $5.23

Ⓑ $4.77   Ⓓ $16.75

43. Estimate by rounding to the nearest tenth. $\begin{array}{r} 6.82 \\ - 5.19 \\ \hline \end{array}$

Ⓐ 2   Ⓒ 1.6

Ⓑ 1   Ⓓ 1.5

44. 2 feet = _____ inches

Ⓐ 6   Ⓒ 12

Ⓑ 36   Ⓓ 24

Pretest

45. 4,000 pounds = _____ tons

   Ⓐ 4   Ⓒ 1,000
   Ⓑ 2   Ⓓ 8

46. 1 pint = _____ cups

   Ⓐ 2   Ⓒ 8
   Ⓑ 4   Ⓓ 16

47. 6 kilometers = _____ meters

   Ⓐ 60   Ⓒ 600
   Ⓑ 60,000   Ⓓ 6,000

48. 1 kilogram = _____ grams

   Ⓐ 1,000   Ⓒ 10,000
   Ⓑ 100   Ⓓ 100,000

49. 7,000 milliliters = _____ liters

   Ⓐ 70   Ⓒ 700
   Ⓑ 7,000   Ⓓ 7

50. Name the figure using symbols.

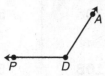

   Ⓐ ∠PAD   Ⓒ ∠PDA
   Ⓑ ∠P   Ⓓ ∠DAP

51. Classify this angle.

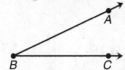

   Ⓐ right   Ⓒ acute
   Ⓑ obtuse   Ⓓ not here

52. Find the perimeter of this rectangle.

   Ⓐ 6 units   Ⓒ 9 units
   Ⓑ 12 units   Ⓓ 10 units

53. Find the perimeter of this rectangle.

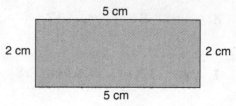

   Ⓐ 14 cm   Ⓒ 10 cm
   Ⓑ 7 cm   Ⓓ 14 square cm

54. Find the area of this rectangle.

   Ⓐ 4 square units   Ⓒ 6 square units
   Ⓑ 5 square units   Ⓓ 4 units

55. Find the area of this rectangle.

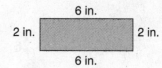

   Ⓐ 12 in.   Ⓒ 12 square in.
   Ⓑ 16 in.   Ⓓ 16 square in.

Using the Pretest Results

After students complete the *Pretest,* compare missed
item numbers to these student book pages.

Item	Page	Item	Page	Item	Page	Item	Page
1	4	15	38	29	78	43	119
2	5	16	40	30	84	44	130
3	8	17	48	31	86	45	131
4	13	18	50	32	88	46	132
5	14	19	52	33	90	47	134
6	18	20	53	34	92	48	136
7	18	21	57	35	94	49	137
8	20	22	60	36	105	50	146
9	20	23	68	37	106	51	146
10	28	24	70	38	108	52	148
11	28	25	74	39	110	53	149
12	30	26	74	40	116	54	150
13	32	27	76	41	119	55	151
14	37	28	76	42	120		

The Language of Mathematics

Vocabulary
difference
digit
estimate
period
place-value chart
regroup
sum
whole number

Building Language
Students work in small groups, using word play to create memory devices for each vocabulary word. Then groups can share their ideas.

Examples:

Fingers are called *digits*. You can use your fingers to count numbers.

Sumo wrestlers are big. The *sum* is bigger than each whole number added.

Assessment
Unit 1 Review, pages 25–27
Unit 1 Test, blackline master, Teacher's Guide, page 14

Working with Whole Numbers · Pages 4–27

Math Skills
Place value, Reading and writing whole numbers, Addition and subtraction, Estimation of sums and differences

Problem-Solving Strategies
Make a graph; Work backwards

Introduction
Materials: newspapers, highlighters
Tell students that, in this unit, they will learn about whole numbers. Ask students to share where and how they used numbers so far that day. Some examples might include telling time, riding the bus to school, or buying lunch. Challenge students to relate numbers to their other classes. Examples: Measuring in science, using dates in social studies, and reading music. Give each student one newspaper page and ask them to highlight every number. Ask students to share the greatest number they found.

Reinforcement Activities
Place Value
Materials: grid paper, pencils, place-value charts
Use this activity to reinforce that a digit's value depends on its place in the number. On the board, write *5,555,555* for students to copy onto their place-value charts. Use multiplication to show each digit's value.
Examples: $5 \times 1 = 5$; $5 \times 10 = 50$; $5 \times 100 = 500$. Ask: *How did the value of each 5 change, moving right to left in the number?*

Addition and Subtraction
Materials: base-ten blocks, paper, pencils
Students work in pairs to model addition and subtraction problems with base-ten blocks. One student models the problem while the other student solves on paper. Then students reverse roles. Remind students how to use inverse operations to check their answers.

Problem-Solving Activities
Make a Graph
Materials: grid paper, pencils
On the board, write the following data in a table: *Mon. 15; Tues. 20; Wed. 20; Thurs. 25; Fri. 30.* Explain that the numbers show the sales of an item for one week and that you want to display the data on a line graph. Ask: *What decisions do you need to make before you draw the line graph?* Lead students to decide a title, labels for both axes, a scale, and intervals. Then help students make the graph.

Work Backwards
Materials: 25 index cards per student pair
Students work in pairs to model working backwards. On the board, write the following problem: *Pat has 13 baseball cards. Carey has 12 baseball cards. Last week, Pat traded 6 cards to Carey for 10 of her cards. How many cards did Carey have before the trade?* One student in each pair is Pat and the other is Carey. Have them use the cards to model the trade backwards. Then students can model forwards to check their answers.

Unit 1 Test

Name _____

1. Write the place name for the 7 in 6,978,235.

   Ⓐ thousands   Ⓒ ten thousands
   Ⓑ millions   Ⓓ hundred thousands

2. Write the value of the underlined digit in 7,698,054.

   Ⓐ 80,000   Ⓒ 800,000
   Ⓑ 80   Ⓓ 8,000

3. Write seven hundred nine thousand, four hundred sixteen using digits.

   Ⓐ 709,416   Ⓒ 79,416
   Ⓑ 790,416   Ⓓ 709,406

4.   342
   + 98

   Ⓐ 330   Ⓒ 440
   Ⓑ 340   Ⓓ 244

5.   746
   + 517

   Ⓐ 1,243   Ⓒ 229
   Ⓑ 1,233   Ⓓ 1,263

6.   3,760
   + 1,249

   Ⓐ 4,009   Ⓒ 4,909
   Ⓑ 5,009   Ⓓ 2,511

7.   278
       79
   + 861

   Ⓐ 1,218   Ⓒ 1,008
   Ⓑ 1,018   Ⓓ 1,208

8.   462
   − 75

   Ⓐ 397   Ⓒ 537
   Ⓑ 497   Ⓓ 387

9.   504
   − 269

   Ⓐ 235   Ⓒ 773
   Ⓑ 335   Ⓓ 245

10.   6,138
    − 2,560

    Ⓐ 8,698   Ⓒ 3,578
    Ⓑ 4,698   Ⓓ 4,678

11.   98,108
    + 27,342

    Ⓐ 115,440   Ⓒ 125,450
    Ⓑ 115,450   Ⓓ 70,766

12.   50,186
    − 31,517

    Ⓐ 18,669   Ⓒ 29,679
    Ⓑ 28,669   Ⓓ 81,703

13. Estimate.   576
              + 322

    Ⓐ 800   Ⓒ 600
    Ⓑ 900   Ⓓ 700

14. Estimate.   8,279
              − 4,361

    Ⓐ 5,000   Ⓒ 4,000
    Ⓑ 2,000   Ⓓ 3,000

The Language of Mathematics

Vocabulary
factor
multiplication
multiply
partial product
product
times

Building Language
It is important to reinforce place value for this unit. Write the following on the board:

Use place-value and multiplication vocabulary to give clues for each blank. Example:

The first factor has three hundreds.

Ask volunteers to come to the board and write the digits. Once all the blanks are filled, ask students to read the problem using the correct vocabulary. Students then find the product. Ask students to identify the partial products.

Multiplication · Pages 28–47

Math Skills
Multiplying by 1-, 2-, and 3-digit numbers, Estimating products

Problem-Solving Strategies
Solve multi-step problems; Identify extra information

Introduction
Materials: pencils, paper
Say: *Four friends each paid $26 for dinner. How much did they pay in all?* Have students first solve by adding $26 + 26 + 26 + 26$. Explain that, like addition, multiplication is combining groups. Then write 4×26 on the board and show students how to find the product. Now say: *Thirty-five people each paid $26 for dinner. How much did they pay in all?* Ask students if they prefer using addition or multiplication to solve and why.

Reinforcement Activities
Multiplying by One Digit
Materials: base-ten blocks
Students work in groups of three. On the board, write 3×587. One student models 500, one models 80, and one models 7 with base-ten blocks. Each student models three times their blocks. Then students combine all the blocks to find the product. Students can then model $587 + 587 + 587$ to check the product.

Partial Products
Materials: lined paper, pencils
When multiplying, students might place the partial products or regrouped numbers in the wrong columns. Write 78×264 on the board. Show students how to use lined paper turned sideways to multiply. Point out that the lines serve as a place-value chart. Students may want to label the columns *H T O* and cross out each regrouped number after it is added.

Problem-Solving Activities
Solve Multi-Step Problems
Explain that, when people write secret codes, the code is more difficult when there are multiple steps. Use this two-step code as an example: The letters in the alphabet correspond to the numbers 1–26 in order. Add 5 to each number. So, the letter *d* would be coded as *9*. To decode, subtract 5 and match the number with its letter. Ask students to use this code to write a message, then to exchange papers and decode.

Identify Extra Information
Materials: the Internet, paper, crayons or colored pencils, highlighters
Students research and write a paragraph about their favorite animal, asking one question at the end. http://www.EnchantedLearning.com/coloring/ has hundreds of printable animal fact sheets, each with a picture of the animal to color. Students then exchange papers and identify the extra information to answer the question. Suggest that students highlight the question for easy reference.

Unit 2 Test

Name _____

1.
$$\begin{array}{r} 73 \\ \times\ 9 \\ \hline \end{array}$$

 Ⓐ 6,321   Ⓒ 657
 Ⓑ 637   Ⓓ 82

2. $3 \times 58 =$ _____

 Ⓐ 174   Ⓒ 61
 Ⓑ 154   Ⓓ 1,524

3.
$$\begin{array}{r} 197 \\ \times\ 6 \\ \hline \end{array}$$

 Ⓐ 1,142   Ⓒ 203
 Ⓑ 1,182   Ⓓ 642

4. $5 \times 428 =$ _____

 Ⓐ 2,040   Ⓒ 2,140
 Ⓑ 2,000   Ⓓ 2,014

5.
$$\begin{array}{r} 83 \\ \times\ 94 \\ \hline \end{array}$$

 Ⓐ 7,802   Ⓒ 177
 Ⓑ 7,712   Ⓓ 1,079

6. Estimate. $16 \times 32 =$ _____

 Ⓐ 600   Ⓒ 500
 Ⓑ 400   Ⓓ 700

7. Estimate.
$$\begin{array}{r} 68 \\ \times\ 23 \\ \hline \end{array}$$

 Ⓐ 1,200   Ⓒ 1,800
 Ⓑ 1,400   Ⓓ 2,100

8.
$$\begin{array}{r} 813 \\ \times\ 47 \\ \hline \end{array}$$

 Ⓐ 860   Ⓒ 38,211
 Ⓑ 953   Ⓓ 37,111

9. $549 \times 51 =$ _____

 Ⓐ 27,990   Ⓒ 600
 Ⓑ 3,294   Ⓓ 27,999

10.
$$\begin{array}{r} 804 \\ \times\ 72 \\ \hline \end{array}$$

 Ⓐ 57,888   Ⓒ 56,880
 Ⓑ 7,236   Ⓓ 876

11. $23 \times 609 =$ _____

 Ⓐ 14,070   Ⓒ 1,407
 Ⓑ 14,700   Ⓓ 14,007

12.
$$\begin{array}{r} 317 \\ \times\ 785 \\ \hline \end{array}$$

 Ⓐ 6,340   Ⓒ 49,135
 Ⓑ 248,845   Ⓓ 1,102

13. $425 \times 193 =$ _____

 Ⓐ 43,775   Ⓒ 5,525
 Ⓑ 618   Ⓓ 82,025

14.
$$\begin{array}{r} 3,549 \\ \times\ 8 \\ \hline \end{array}$$

 Ⓐ 24,022   Ⓒ 28,392
 Ⓑ 24,392   Ⓓ 3,557

15. $20 \times 52,896 =$ _____

 Ⓐ 104,682   Ⓒ 105,792
 Ⓑ 1,046,820   Ⓓ 1,057,920

16.
$$\begin{array}{r} 8,752 \\ \times\ 49 \\ \hline \end{array}$$

 Ⓐ 428,848   Ⓒ 113,776
 Ⓑ 482,848   Ⓓ 113,767

The Language of Mathematics

Vocabulary
divide
dividend
divisor
place holder
quotient
remainder
trial quotient

Building Language
Materials: paper, pencils

Write the following on the board for students to copy on their papers:

```
   64 R5
7)453
 − 42↓
   33
 − 28
    5
```

Then challenge students to check the division and label each part of the multiplication with the division vocabulary: *dividend, divisor, quotient, and remainder.*

```
   64  ← quotient
×   7  ← divisor
 448
+   5  ← remainder
 453  ← dividend
```

Assessment
Unit 3 Review, pages 65–67
Unit 3 Test, blackline master, Teacher's Guide, page 18

Division • Pages 48–67

Math Skills
Dividing by 1- and 2-digit numbers, Trial quotients, Estimating quotients

Problem-Solving Strategies
Choose an operation; Write a number sentence

Introduction
Materials: paper, pencils
Remind students that multiplication is repeated addition. Then show that division is repeated subtraction. Say: *I have 96 cookies. I will give 8 to each of my students. How many students do I have?* Students can first solve by subtracting $96 − 8$ until they reach 0. Ask: *How many times did you subtract groups of 8 cookies?* Then write $96 ÷ 8$ and show students how to find the quotient. Ask which method they prefer. Explain that they can use repeated subtraction to check their division.

Reinforcement Activities
Division
Materials: number cubes, paper, pencils
Explain the whole number divisibility rules for 2, 5, and 10. *If the number is even, it is divisible by 2. If the ones digit is a 5 or 0, it is divisible by 5. If the ones digit is 0, the number is divisible by 10.* Tell students that they can use these rules to check their quotients. For example, if they get a remainder for $635 ÷ 5$, then there is an error in the division. Students can work in pairs to test numbers for divisibility by 2, 5, and 10. Taking turns rolling the cube, students write several 3- and 4-digit numbers. Have them use the divisibility rules, then divide to check. Ask students to share their results. You may want to share the divisibility rules for 3, 6, and 9.

Trial Quotients
Materials: paper, pencils
Explain that, in each step of division, students use estimation to choose a trial quotient. Write $4,934 ÷ 8$ on the board. Estimate the quotient first as $4,800 ÷ 8 = 600$. Then point out the estimates used while showing the division. Students can work in pairs to estimate and solve several division problems. Ask: *How does estimating the quotient first help you divide?*

Problem-Solving Activities
Choose an Operation
Divide the class into four groups and assign each group an operation. Ask students to brainstorm a list of words in a problem that might be used to indicate their operation. Give a few examples, such as *in all* for addition and *fewer* for subtraction. Then groups can share their lists.

Write a Number Sentence
Materials: paper, pencils
Students work in pairs. Have each student write four number sentences, one for each operation. Then have students trade papers and write the inverse of each operation's number sentence. For example: $63 ÷ 9 = 7$ and $9 × 7 = 63$. Students may check each other's work.

Unit 3 Test

1. $81 \div 3 =$ _____
- Ⓐ 2 R7
- Ⓑ 17
- Ⓒ 26
- Ⓓ 27

2. $4\overline{)144}$
- Ⓐ 35
- Ⓑ 34
- Ⓒ 37
- Ⓓ 36

3. $654 \div 3 =$ _____
- Ⓐ 21
- Ⓑ 218
- Ⓒ 281
- Ⓓ 28

4. $7\overline{)4,207}$
- Ⓐ 61
- Ⓑ 601
- Ⓒ 610
- Ⓓ 60

5. $97 \div 5 =$ _____
- Ⓐ 18
- Ⓑ 18 R2
- Ⓒ 19
- Ⓓ 19 R2

6. $9\overline{)681}$
- Ⓐ 74 R6
- Ⓑ 74 R1
- Ⓒ 75 R6
- Ⓓ 75 R1

7. $3,218 \div 8 =$ _____
- Ⓐ 420 R2
- Ⓑ 40 R2
- Ⓒ 402 R2
- Ⓓ 42 R2

8. Estimate. $6\overline{)375}$
- Ⓐ 60
- Ⓑ 50
- Ⓒ 70
- Ⓓ 80

9. Estimate. $4\overline{)756}$
- Ⓐ 200
- Ⓑ 100
- Ⓒ 20
- Ⓓ 300

10. $20\overline{)760}$
- Ⓐ 38
- Ⓑ 39
- Ⓒ 37
- Ⓓ 36

11. $431 \div 50 =$ _____
- Ⓐ 83 R1
- Ⓑ 8 R1
- Ⓒ 8 R31
- Ⓓ 8 R3

12. $14\overline{)406}$
- Ⓐ 27
- Ⓑ 209
- Ⓒ 28 R4
- Ⓓ 29

13. $75\overline{)600}$
- Ⓐ 7 R5
- Ⓑ 80
- Ⓒ 7
- Ⓓ 8

14. $9,296 \div 56 =$ _____
- Ⓐ 16
- Ⓑ 16 R6
- Ⓒ 166
- Ⓓ 106

15. $32\overline{)847}$
- Ⓐ 26 R15
- Ⓑ 25 R1
- Ⓒ 26 R5
- Ⓓ 216 R5

16. $1,653 \div 79 =$ _____
- Ⓐ 20 R73
- Ⓑ 27 R3
- Ⓒ 20 R3
- Ⓓ 2 R73

17. Estimate. $21\overline{)587}$
- Ⓐ 30
- Ⓑ 40
- Ⓒ 50
- Ⓓ 20

18. Estimate. $48\overline{)296}$
- Ⓐ 60
- Ⓑ 6
- Ⓒ 80
- Ⓓ 8

The Language of Mathematics

Vocabulary
denominator
equivalent fraction
estimate
fraction
higher terms
improper fraction
mixed number
number line
numerator
round
simplest terms

Building Language
Materials: 11 index cards per student, pencils, highlighters

Have students draw an example of each vocabulary word on one side of each card and write the word on the other side. Remind students that they might need to draw an arrow or highlight the word in their examples.

Then students can work in pairs, using the index cards as flash cards to name each drawing.

Assessment
Unit 4 Review, pages 101–103
Unit 4 Test, blackline master, Teacher's Guide, page 20

Fractions • Pages 68–103

Math Skills
Reading and writing fractions, Equivalent fractions, Comparing and ordering fractions, Improper fractions, Mixed numbers, Adding and subtracting fractions, mixed numbers, and whole numbers, Estimating fractions

Problem-Solving Strategies
Use logic; Make a model

Introduction
Count the number of students in the class. Write the number on the board. Explain that the denominator of a fraction represents the whole, or the total number, in a group. Then ask questions for the numerators, such as how many students have dogs. Explain that this count is the numerator, or the part of the whole you want to represent. Have students work in small groups to name and describe other fractions.

Reinforcement Activities
Equivalent Fractions
Materials: paper, crayons or colored pencils
Instruct students to fold a piece of paper in half and shade one half of it. Ask what fraction of the paper is shaded. Have them fold the paper again to show that $\frac{1}{2} = \frac{2}{4}$. Students can then fold the paper one last time to show that $\frac{1}{2} = \frac{2}{4} = \frac{4}{8}$. Write the equivalent fractions on the board. This activity can be repeated with $\frac{1}{3}$.

Adding and Subtracting Fractions and Mixed Numbers
Materials: inch rulers, paper, pencils
Show students how to use a ruler to add and subtract fractions and mixed numbers with denominators of 2, 4, 8, and 16. For $1\frac{1}{4} + \frac{1}{2}$, tell students to draw a line $1\frac{1}{4}$ inches long. Have them extend the line by $\frac{1}{2}$ inch without moving the ruler. Ask: *At what point does your line end now?* Give another example with subtraction. Then students may practice on their own and check their work by finding the sums and differences on paper.

Problem-Solving Activities
Use Logic
Materials: paper, pencils
Write the following on the board: *I am thinking of a mixed number between 2 and 3. When renamed as an improper fraction, it has a denominator of 4. What number am I thinking of?* Students can work in small groups to use logic to find two possible answers. Then challenge students to write their own fraction or mixed number logic puzzle to share with the class.

Make a Model
Materials: fraction strips; 10 fraction cards per student pair
Students work in pairs to model fractions. Give each student pair 10 index cards with different fractions written on them. Each student shuffles the cards and takes one to model with strips. Then students can use the models to compare, add, and subtract their fractions.

Unit 4 Test

1. Write four ninths as a fraction.
   - (A) $\frac{4}{9}$
   - (C) $4\frac{1}{9}$
   - (B) $\frac{9}{4}$
   - (D) 4.9

2. Write the word name for $\frac{5}{8}$.
   - (A) five eight
   - (C) five and eight
   - (B) fifty-eight
   - (D) five eighths

3. Write $\frac{48}{8}$ as a whole number.
   - (A) 40
   - (C) 8
   - (B) 6
   - (D) 7

4. Write $\frac{26}{3}$ as a mixed number.
   - (A) $6\frac{2}{3}$
   - (C) $8\frac{2}{3}$
   - (B) $6\frac{1}{3}$
   - (D) $8\frac{1}{2}$

5. Write $7\frac{2}{3}$ as an improper fraction.
   - (A) $\frac{21}{3}$
   - (C) $\frac{23}{7}$
   - (B) $\frac{23}{3}$
   - (D) $\frac{23}{2}$

6. Which fraction is equivalent to $\frac{2}{5}$?
   - (A) $\frac{2}{10}$
   - (C) $\frac{4}{10}$
   - (B) $\frac{1}{5}$
   - (D) $\frac{4}{5}$

7. Simplify. $\frac{6}{42} =$ _____
   - (A) $\frac{2}{23}$
   - (C) $\frac{1}{37}$
   - (B) $\frac{1}{6}$
   - (D) $\frac{1}{7}$

8. Add and simplify. $\frac{3}{5} + \frac{1}{5} =$ _____
   - (A) $\frac{2}{5}$
   - (C) $\frac{4}{5}$
   - (B) $\frac{3}{10}$
   - (D) $\frac{4}{10}$

9. Subtract and simplify. $\frac{6}{7} - \frac{3}{7} =$ _____
   - (A) $\frac{3}{7}$
   - (C) $\frac{9}{7}$
   - (B) $\frac{3}{14}$
   - (D) $\frac{7}{3}$

10. Add and simplify. $5\frac{1}{4} + 3\frac{2}{4} =$ _____
    - (A) $5\frac{3}{4}$
    - (C) $2\frac{3}{4}$
    - (B) $8\frac{3}{8}$
    - (D) $8\frac{3}{4}$

11. Subtract and simplify. $10\frac{5}{6} - 6\frac{1}{6} =$ _____
    - (A) $10\frac{2}{3}$
    - (C) $4\frac{2}{3}$
    - (B) $10\frac{4}{6}$
    - (D) $6\frac{4}{6}$

12. Add and simplify. $\frac{3}{8} + \frac{2}{8} =$ _____
    - (A) $\frac{4}{12}$
    - (C) $\frac{1}{3}$
    - (B) $\frac{5}{8}$
    - (D) $\frac{4}{8}$

13. Subtract and simplify. $\frac{7}{10} - \frac{5}{10} =$ _____
    - (A) $\frac{6}{10}$
    - (C) $\frac{3}{5}$
    - (B) $\frac{1}{5}$
    - (D) $\frac{6}{2}$

14. Add and simplify. $5\frac{1}{3} + 2\frac{1}{5} =$ _____
    - (A) $7\frac{2}{8}$
    - (C) $7\frac{1}{4}$
    - (B) $7\frac{8}{15}$
    - (D) $\frac{8}{15}$

15. Subtract and simplify. $9\frac{1}{4} - 5\frac{2}{5} =$ _____
    - (A) $3\frac{17}{20}$
    - (C) $4\frac{17}{20}$
    - (B) $4\frac{3}{20}$
    - (D) $14\frac{13}{20}$

16. Subtract and simplify. $4 - 2\frac{1}{3} =$ _____
    - (A) $2\frac{1}{3}$
    - (C) $1\frac{2}{3}$
    - (B) $2\frac{2}{3}$
    - (D) 2

Decimals · Pages 104–129

Math Skills
Reading, writing, and rounding decimals, Comparing and ordering decimals, Fraction and decimal equivalents, Adding and subtracting decimals, Estimating decimal sums and differences

Problem-Solving Strategies
Find a pattern; Use estimation

Introduction
Materials: rulers, pencils
Explain that, like fractions, decimals are numbers between whole numbers. Lead students to brainstorm a list of real-world situations where they have seen or used decimals. Some examples might include shopping, weather forecasts, and sports. Ask students why they think that decimals are sometimes preferred over fractions.

Reinforcement Activities
Compare and Order Decimals
Materials: 10 × 10 grid paper, crayons or colored pencils
Students work in groups of three to compare and order decimals. Write *0.5, 0.05,* and *0.55* on the board. Each student in the group shades one grid to represent one of the decimals. Then groups can use the grids to order the decimals from least to greatest.

Adding and Subtracting Decimals
Materials: meter sticks, pencils, paper
Explain that 1 meter is divided into 10 decimeters, 100 centimeters, and 1,000 millimeters. Write the following on the board: *1 dm = 0.1 m; 1 cm = 0.01 m; 1 mm = 0.001 m.* Show students how to use a meter stick to add decimals. For 0.35 + 0.8, draw a line 35 centimeters long. Without moving the ruler, extend the line 8 decimeters. Ask: *At what point does your line end now?* Give another example with subtraction.

Problem-Solving Activities
Find a Pattern
Materials: rulers, pencils
Have students draw a 10-inch number line, label the ends *0* and *1,* and divide it into ten sections. Point out that, since there are ten equal parts, each part is $\frac{1}{10}$ of the whole. Have students label the sections $\frac{1}{10}, \frac{2}{10}, \dots \frac{9}{10}$. Then add a second label line for those fractions that can be simplified and a third label line for the decimal equivalents. Ask students to describe the patterns they see on their number lines.

Use Estimation
Materials: play money, paper, pencils
Write the following amounts on the board: *$4.67, $0.23, $0.08.* Tell students to model each amount with play money. Then ask students which one coin or bill is closest in value to those amounts. Ask: *To what place value did you round each amount?* Have students estimate the sum of these amounts and compare it to the exact sum.

Unit 5 Test

Name _____

1. Write twelve thousandths as a decimal.
   - (A) 12,000
   - (B) 1.200
   - (C) 0.12
   - (D) 0.012

2. Write eight dollars and twenty-one cents using a dollar sign and a decimal point.
   - (A) $8.21
   - (B) $8.20
   - (C) $80.21
   - (D) $82.10

3. Compare.   3.48 _____ 34.8
   Write <, >, or =.
   - (A) <
   - (B) >
   - (C) =
   - (D) not here

4. Compare.   6.09 _____ 6.090
   Write <, >, or =.
   - (A) <
   - (B) >
   - (C) =
   - (D) not here

5. Write 0.09 as a fraction.
   - (A) $\frac{1}{9}$
   - (B) $\frac{9}{10}$
   - (C) $\frac{9}{100}$
   - (D) $\frac{90}{100}$

6. Write 2.07 as a mixed number.
   - (A) $2\frac{1}{7}$
   - (B) $2\frac{7}{100}$
   - (C) $2\frac{7}{10}$
   - (D) $\frac{2}{7}$

7. Write $\frac{4}{5}$ as a decimal.
   - (A) 4.5
   - (B) 0.8
   - (C) 5.4
   - (D) 0.08

8. Write $3\frac{1}{2}$ as a decimal.
   - (A) 3.2
   - (B) 0.32
   - (C) 3.5
   - (D) 0.35

9. Round $7.63 to the nearest whole dollar.
   - (A) $8
   - (B) $6
   - (C) $7.60
   - (D) $7

10.
    $$4.69 + 2.05$$
    - (A) 6.74
    - (B) 0.674
    - (C) 2.64
    - (D) 67.4

11.
    $$25.8 + 3.921$$
    - (A) 297.21
    - (B) 21.879
    - (C) 29.721
    - (D) 2.9721

12.
    $$40 - 8.35$$
    - (A) 40.835
    - (B) 31.75
    - (C) 42.75
    - (D) 31.65

13.
    $$\$10.08 - 7.29$$
    - (A) $2.79
    - (B) $27.90
    - (C) $17.37
    - (D) $2.81

14. Estimate by rounding to the nearest one. $27.31 + 5.69
    - (A) $30
    - (B) $34
    - (C) $33
    - (D) $32

15. Estimate by rounding to the nearest tenth.   34.75 − 10.41
    - (A) 24
    - (B) 2
    - (C) 24.4
    - (D) 2.44

The Language of Mathematics

Vocabulary
capacity
centimeter
cup
foot
gallon
gram
inch
kilogram
kilometer
liter
mass
meter
mile
milliliter
millimeter
ounce
pint
pound
quart
ton
yard

Building Language
Materials: index cards

Write the customary and metric measurements on cards and pass them out to the class. First ask students to group themselves into customary or metric measurements. Then have them group as *length, weight/mass,* or *capacity.* Finally ask customary students to find their closest metric match. Discuss the matches with the class.

Assessment
Unit 6 Review, pages 143–145
Unit 6 Test, blackline master, Teacher's Guide, page 24

Measurement • Pages 130–145

Math Skills
Customary length, weight, and capacity, Metric length, mass, and capacity, Relating and comparing measurements

Problem-Solving Strategy
Guess and check

Introduction
Materials: inch ruler, meter stick, 1-lb weight, 1-kg weight, measuring cup, 1-liter bottle
Divide the board into six columns and label them with each object in the materials list. Allow students to handle the objects. Then students can work together in small groups to list objects around the classroom that are close to, much less than, or much greater than each measure. Ask groups to share their lists.

Reinforcement Activities
Customary Capacity
Materials: cup, pint, quart, and gallon containers, beans
Students work in groups of four. First, ask students to use only the cup to fill the larger three containers with beans, then only the pint, and finally the quart. Allow students to use the containers to find the number of cups, pints, and quarts in one gallon. Challenge students to describe how to use the quart container to measure one cup.

Metric Mass
Materials: paper clips, metric scale, various small objects to weigh
Give each group of students 100 paper clips and a scale. Have them weigh one paper clip to see that it is about 1 gram. Then students can hold a small object, such as an eraser, in one hand and the paper clip in the other to compare their weights. Ask: *How many paper clips would equal the weight of the eraser?* Then students can use the scale to test their estimates.

Relating Customary and Metric Length
Materials: yardsticks, meter sticks
Students work in pairs to estimate and measure customary and metric lengths. Ask one student in each pair to hold his or her hands about one inch apart. Partners can check the estimate by measuring the space. Ask a volunteer to draw a 1-inch line on the board and label it. Do the same for *foot* and *yard.* Then repeat the activity for *meter, centimeter,* and *millimeter.* Ask students to look at the lines on the board and discuss the differences.

Problem-Solving Activities
Guess and Check
Materials: inch rulers, yardsticks, paper, pencils
Instruct students to divide their papers into three columns labeled *Object, Guess,* and *Check.* Students work in pairs. First, ask students to estimate each other's heights, then the lengths of each other's hair, arms, legs, fingers, and feet. Record the estimates in the *Guess* column. Students can measure to check and then record their measurements in the *Check* column.

Unit 6 Test

Name _____

1. 24 inches = _____ feet
    - (A) 1
    - (B) 2
    - (C) 3
    - (D) 4

2. 64 ounces = _____ pounds
    - (A) 16
    - (B) 2
    - (C) 32
    - (D) 4

3. 5 gallons = _____ cups
    - (A) 4
    - (B) 80
    - (C) 40
    - (D) 8

4. 10,560 feet = _____ miles
    - (A) 10
    - (B) 3
    - (C) 2
    - (D) 5

5. 10 pounds = _____ ounces
    - (A) 16
    - (B) 1.6
    - (C) 160
    - (D) 1,600

6. 75 feet = _____ yards
    - (A) 225
    - (B) 7.5
    - (C) 25
    - (D) 900

7. Compare. 2 tons _____ 2,000 pounds
    Write <, >, or =.
    - (A) <
    - (B) >
    - (C) =
    - (D) not here

8. Compare. 8 pints _____ 2 quarts
    Write <, >, or =.
    - (A) <
    - (B) >
    - (C) =
    - (D) not here

9. 400 centimeters = _____ meters
    - (A) 40
    - (B) 4
    - (C) 400
    - (D) 4,000

10. 2 kilometers = _____ meters
    - (A) 2,000
    - (B) 20,000
    - (C) 20
    - (D) 200

11. 1.5 kilograms = _____ grams
    - (A) 15
    - (B) 15,000
    - (C) 1,500
    - (D) 150

12. 1,800 milliliters = _____ liters
    - (A) 1.8
    - (B) 0.18
    - (C) 18
    - (D) 180

13. Which is the best measurement for the weight of a dictionary?
    - (A) 5 g
    - (B) 5 kg
    - (C) 50 lb
    - (D) 5 oz

14. Which is the best measurement for the length of a bus?
    - (A) 20 m
    - (B) 2 m
    - (C) 2 cm
    - (D) 200 mm

15. Compare. 15 cm _____ 1,500 mm
    Write <, >, or =.
    - (A) <
    - (B) >
    - (C) =
    - (D) not here

16. Compare. 3,800 mL _____ 38 L
    Write <, >, or =.
    - (A) <
    - (B) >
    - (C) =
    - (D) not here

The Language of Mathematics

Vocabulary
acute angle
angle
area
degrees
formula
obtuse angle
perimeter
point
ray
right angle
square units

Building Language
Materials: newspapers, magazines

Students look through newspapers and magazines for pictures to illustrate geometry vocabulary. Challenge students to choose one picture to illustrate as many words as possible. For example, a football field may show *angles*, *perimeter*, *area*, *point*, and *square units*.

Ask students to label their pictures with the vocabulary words and display them in the classroom.

Assessment
Unit 7 Review, pages 155–156
Unit 7 Test, blackline master, Teacher's Guide, page 26

Geometry • Pages 146–156

Math Skills
Angles, Perimeter, Area

Problem-Solving Strategy
Use a formula

Introduction
Review basic plane figures with students. Ask students to identify examples of each figure. Point out that the classroom floor is a rectangle. Tell students to describe its corners. Then ask students to estimate how much rope they would need to go around the classroom and how much carpet they would need to cover the entire floor. Explain that, in this unit, they will learn about describing and measuring the spaces around them.

Reinforcement Activities
Angles
Materials: protractors, pencils, paper, overhead projector
First show students how to use two pencils to make angles. Ask students to hold up their pencils in the shapes of acute, obtuse, and right angles. Explain that a protractor is a tool students can use to draw exact angles. Use the protractor on the overhead projector to draw several angles. Then ask students to use their protractors to draw 90°, 35°, and 140° angles.

Perimeter
Materials: 16 connecting cubes per student
Ask students to arrange the 16 cubes into as many rectangles as they can, using all the cubes each time. Have students write the perimeter and area of each rectangle. Students will see that all the rectangles have the same area. Ask which rectangle has the smallest perimeter and what kind of rectangle it is. Repeat the activity with 4 cubes, 9 cubes, or 25 cubes. This activity introduces the relationship between perimeter and area and demonstrates the unique properties of squares and square numbers.

Area
Materials: cardboard, inch and centimeter rulers, scissors
Show students how to measure and cut a 1-cm square, 1-in. square, and 1-ft square of cardboard. Then ask students to use the squares to measure the area of their desks, notebooks, the chalkboard or bulletin board, and the classroom floor. Students can share and compare their measurements with the class.

Problem-Solving Activities
Use a Formula
Materials: paper, pencils
Remind students that they used formulas in Unit 6 to change units of measurement. Challenge students to choose three changes of measurement to write as a formula. For example, to change feet to inches, they could use the formula $i = f \times 12$. Then students can work in groups to test each other's formulas.

Unit 7 Test

1. Name this angle using symbols.

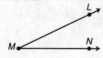

- Ⓐ ∠MNL
- Ⓒ ∠LMN
- Ⓑ ∠N
- Ⓓ ∠LM

2. Name this angle using symbols.

- Ⓐ ∠Y
- Ⓒ ∠Z
- Ⓑ ∠WYZ
- Ⓓ ∠YWZ

3. Classify this angle.

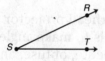

- Ⓐ right
- Ⓒ acute
- Ⓑ obtuse
- Ⓓ not here

4. Which angle is obtuse?

5. Classify the angles inside this triangle.

- Ⓐ right
- Ⓒ acute
- Ⓑ obtuse
- Ⓓ not here

6. Find the perimeter of this rectangle.

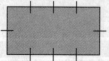

- Ⓐ 8 units
- Ⓒ 10 units
- Ⓑ 12 units
- Ⓓ 14 units

7. Find the perimeter of this rectangle.

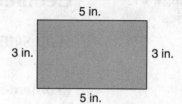

- Ⓐ 15 in.
- Ⓒ 14 in.
- Ⓑ 12 in.
- Ⓓ 16 in.

8. Find the perimeter of this rectangle.

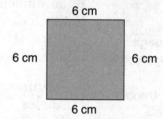

- Ⓐ 36 cm
- Ⓒ 24 cm
- Ⓑ 12 cm
- Ⓓ 20 cm

9. Find the area of this rectangle.

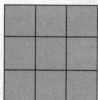

- Ⓐ 12 square units
- Ⓒ 6 units
- Ⓑ 9 square units
- Ⓓ 12 units

10. Find the area of this rectangle.

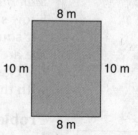

- Ⓐ 80 m
- Ⓒ 80 square meters
- Ⓑ 18 meters
- Ⓓ 36 square meters

Mastery Test

1. Write the value of the underlined digit in 75,6<u>3</u>9,108.

   (A) 30,000　　　(C) 300,000
   (B) 3,000　　　 (D) 3,000,000

2. Write six million, eighty-five thousand, one hundred twenty using digits.

   (A) 6,085,102　　(C) 6,085,120
   (B) 6,850,102　　(D) 6,850,120

3. Add.　　　6,274
   　　　　 + 652

   (A) 5,622　　　(C) 6,826
   (B) 6,296　　　(D) 6,926

4. Add.　　　　458
   　　　　　　196
   　　　　 + 204

   (A) 848　　　(C) 748
   (B) 758　　　(D) 858

5. Subtract.　　963
   　　　　　 − 254

   (A) 1,217　　　(C) 709
   (B) 719　　　 (D) 79

6. Subtract.　36,804
   　　　　 − 17,563

   (A) 19,241　　(C) 19,361
   (B) 54,367　　(D) 21,341

7. Add.　　　65,207
   　　　　 + 2,895

   (A) 67,092　　(C) 63,102
   (B) 68,102　　(D) 62,312

8. Estimate.　4,165
   　　　　　 + 316

   (A) 4,400　　(C) 4,600
   (B) 4,000　　(D) 4,500

9. Estimate.　　713
   　　　　　 − 269

   (A) 600　　　(C) 500
   (B) 400　　　(D) 300

10. Multiply.　　76
    　　　　　 × 5

    (A) 350　　　(C) 305
    (B) 81　　　 (D) 380

11. Multiply. $6 \times 324 =$ ____

    (A) 330　　　(C) 1,944
    (B) 1,824　　(D) 1,924

12. Multiply.　906
    　　　　　 × 3

    (A) 2,718　　(C) 909
    (B) 2,781　　(D) 2,708

13. Multiply. $49 \times 538 =$ ____

    (A) 25,632　　(C) 587
    (B) 26,362　　(D) 6,994

14. Estimate.　　76
    　　　　　 × 29

    (A) 1,400　　(C) 2,400
    (B) 7,000　　(D) 2,100

Mastery Test

Name _____

15. Multiply. 453
            $\times\ 750$

Ⓐ 1,203   Ⓒ 339,750
Ⓑ 5,436   Ⓓ 33,975

16. Multiply. $83 \times 1,609 =$ _____

Ⓐ 133,547   Ⓒ 1,692
Ⓑ 13,547   Ⓓ 17,699

17. Divide. $483 \div 7 =$ _____

Ⓐ 6 R9   Ⓒ 69
Ⓑ 96   Ⓓ 68 R6

18. Divide. $3\overline{)161}$

Ⓐ 5 R3   Ⓒ 530 R2
Ⓑ 54   Ⓓ 53 R2

19. Divide. $2\overline{)615}$

Ⓐ 307 R1   Ⓒ 307
Ⓑ 37 R1   Ⓓ 370 R1

20. Divide. $60\overline{)5,880}$

Ⓐ 98   Ⓒ 980
Ⓑ 89   Ⓓ 908

21. Estimate. $8\overline{)632}$

Ⓐ 80   Ⓒ 8
Ⓑ 90   Ⓓ 9

22. Estimate. $32\overline{)879}$

Ⓐ 3   Ⓒ 20
Ⓑ 30   Ⓓ 4

23. Divide. $17\overline{)9,214}$

Ⓐ 520 R4   Ⓒ 540 R2
Ⓑ 524   Ⓓ 542

24. Write seven tenths as a fraction.

Ⓐ $\frac{1}{7}$ Ⓒ $\frac{7}{100}$
Ⓑ $\frac{7}{10}$ Ⓓ $7\frac{1}{10}$

25. Write $\frac{63}{9}$ as a whole number.

Ⓐ 9   Ⓒ 6
Ⓑ 8   Ⓓ 7

26. Write an equivalent fraction for $\frac{1}{3}$.

Ⓐ $\frac{2}{3}$ Ⓒ $\frac{3}{4}$
Ⓑ $\frac{2}{6}$ Ⓓ $\frac{3}{6}$

27. Write $\frac{37}{9}$ as a mixed number.

Ⓐ $\frac{1}{9}$ Ⓒ $1\frac{1}{9}$
Ⓑ $1\frac{1}{3}$ Ⓓ $4\frac{1}{9}$

28. Write $8\frac{2}{3}$ as an improper fraction.

Ⓐ $\frac{10}{3}$ Ⓒ $\frac{24}{3}$
Ⓑ $\frac{26}{3}$ Ⓓ $\frac{13}{3}$

29. Add. Simplify. $\frac{1}{5} + \frac{3}{5} =$ _____

Ⓐ $\frac{2}{5}$ Ⓒ $\frac{4}{10}$
Ⓑ $\frac{1}{5}$ Ⓓ $\frac{4}{5}$

30. Subtract. Simplify. $\frac{6}{11} - \frac{4}{11} =$ _____

Ⓐ $\frac{2}{11}$ Ⓒ $\frac{10}{11}$
Ⓑ $\frac{3}{11}$ Ⓓ $\frac{8}{22}$

Mastery Test

Name _____

31. Subtract. Simplify. $8\frac{5}{7} - 7\frac{1}{7} = $ _____

(A) 1   (C) $1\frac{4}{7}$

(B) $1\frac{6}{7}$ (D) $\frac{4}{7}$

32. Add. Simplify. $\frac{2}{3} + \frac{6}{7} = $ _____

(A) $\frac{8}{10}$ (C) $\frac{4}{5}$

(B) $\frac{4}{21}$ (D) $1\frac{11}{21}$

33. Subtract. Simplify. $\frac{7}{8} - \frac{3}{4} = $ _____

(A) $\frac{1}{8}$ (C) 4

(B) $\frac{3}{8}$ (D) $\frac{1}{2}$

34. Add. Simplify. $4\frac{1}{6} + 3\frac{1}{3} = $ _____

(A) $1\frac{2}{3}$ (C) $7\frac{2}{3}$

(B) $7\frac{1}{2}$ (D) $7\frac{1}{3}$

35. Add. Simplify. $5\frac{1}{5} + 2\frac{1}{2} = $ _____

(A) $7\frac{2}{7}$ (C) $7\frac{2}{5}$

(B) $7\frac{7}{10}$ (D) $7\frac{3}{7}$

36. Subtract. Simplify. $6\frac{1}{2} - 4\frac{1}{4} = $ _____

(A) $6\frac{1}{2}$ (C) $6\frac{1}{4}$

(B) $2\frac{1}{2}$ (D) $2\frac{1}{4}$

37. Subtract. Simplify. $7 - 2\frac{3}{5} = $ _____

(A) $5\frac{4}{5}$ (C) $5\frac{2}{5}$

(B) $4\frac{2}{5}$ (D) 5

38. Write the value of the underlined digit in 14.3<u>5</u>9.

(A) 3 tenths   (C) 3 thousandths

(B) 3 hundredths   (D) 3 tens

39. Write one hundred four thousandths as a decimal.

(A) 104,000   (C) 104

(B) 0.14   (D) 0.104

40. Compare.   5.36 _____ 5.036
Write <, >, or =.

(A) <   (C) =

(B) >   (D) not here

41. Write 0.009 as a fraction.

(A) $\frac{1}{9}$ (C) $\frac{9}{10}$

(B) $\frac{9}{1,000}$ (D) $\frac{9}{100}$

42. Add. $\begin{array}{r} 5.43 \\ + 2.09 \\ \hline \end{array}$

(A) 7.52   (C) 3.34

(B) 0.752   (D) 75.2

43. Estimate by rounding to the nearest one. $\begin{array}{r} 27.8 \\ + 1.6 \\ \hline \end{array}$

(A) 30   (C) 28

(B) 31   (D) 29

44. Estimate by rounding to the nearest tenth. $\begin{array}{r} 67.28 \\ + 15.21 \\ \hline \end{array}$

(A) 82   (C) 52.1

(B) 52.4   (D) 82.5

45. Subtract. $\begin{array}{r} \$15.03 \\ - 4.38 \\ \hline \end{array}$

(A) $1.65   (C) $19.41

(B) $11.35   (D) $10.65

Mastery Test

46. Estimate by rounding to the nearest tenth. 10.32
                                    − 4.19

  Ⓐ 6   Ⓒ 6.1
  Ⓑ 7   Ⓓ 7.1

47. 3 feet = _____ inches

  Ⓐ 12   Ⓒ 1
  Ⓑ 36   Ⓓ 24

48. 5 tons = _____ pounds

  Ⓐ 10,000   Ⓒ 5,000
  Ⓑ 2,000   Ⓓ 5

49. 2 quarts = _____ pints

  Ⓐ 1   Ⓒ 4
  Ⓑ 2   Ⓓ 8

50. 8 centimeters = _____ millimeters

  Ⓐ 8   Ⓒ 800
  Ⓑ 80   Ⓓ 8,000

51. 90,000 grams = _____ kilograms

  Ⓐ 9,000   Ⓒ 9
  Ⓑ 900   Ⓓ 90

52. 20 liters = _____ milliliters

  Ⓐ 2   Ⓒ 200
  Ⓑ 20,000   Ⓓ 2,000

53. Classify this angle.

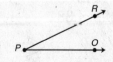

  Ⓐ right   Ⓒ acute
  Ⓑ obtuse   Ⓓ not here

54. Find the perimeter of this rectangle.

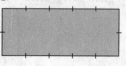

  Ⓐ 7 units   Ⓒ 12 units
  Ⓑ 10 units   Ⓓ 14 units

55. Find the perimeter of this rectangle.

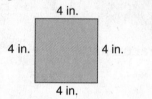

  Ⓐ 8 in.   Ⓒ 16 in.
  Ⓑ 20 in.   Ⓓ 12 in.

56. Find the area of this rectangle.

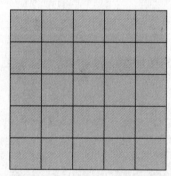

  Ⓐ 20 square units   Ⓒ 10 square units
  Ⓑ 25 square units   Ⓓ 25 units

57. Find the area of this rectangle.

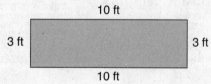

  Ⓐ 13 square ft   Ⓒ 30 square ft
  Ⓑ 26 square ft   Ⓓ 16 ft

UNIT 1
Page 4

	hundred millions	ten millions	millions	hundred thousands	ten thousands	thousands	hundreds	tens	ones
1.	3	6	6,	7	8	9,	3	0	2
2.			2,	3	0	4,	3	6	1
3.		1	9,	0	7	6,	5	4	1
4.			8,	8	5	4,	6	3	2
5.					9	7,	0	6	5
6.			8,	0	0	5,	0	0	2

	a	b
7.	tens	ten thousands
8.	hundred thousands	millions
9.	hundreds	ones
10.	thousands	ten millions

	a	b
11.	0 thousands	8 tens
12.	8 ten millions	4 millions
13.	4 hundred thousands	5 ones
14.	1 hundred million	0 hundreds

Page 5

	a	b	c
1.	758,493	6,473,829	868,582
2.	2,030,200	5,000,400	6,050,407
3.	30,782	406,702	3,908,454

4.	720,462
5.	25,201
6.	184,039
7.	100,243,000
8.	210,612
9.	10,000,275

10. sixteen thousand, three hundred forty-nine
11. seven hundred seventy-six
12. sixteen
13. one hundred twenty-three thousand, four hundred fifty-six

Page 6

	a	b	c	d
1.	844	617	1,203	1,390
2.	1,153	1,160	1,118	1,697
3.	721	613	905	841
4.	441	551	661	521

Page 7

	a	b	c	d	e
1.	823	843	316	432	962
2.	501	598	400	814	428
3.	1,250	400	1,319	816	708
4.	1,570	1,186	560	822	811
5.	820	344	1,542	1,123	943

	a	b	c
6.	1,037	500	1,405
7.	1,571	1,649	230

Mixed Practice

	a	b
1.	8 thousands	4 millions
2.	173,112	
3.	2,061,025	

Page 8

	a	b	c	d
1.	4,146	9,385	9,247	8,835
2.	5,015	9,813	8,415	9,491
3.	10,312	7,584	7,883	6,789
4.	8,874	4,678	9,360	8,013

Page 9

	a	b	c	d	e
1.	8,033	6,413	7,520	9,229	2,638
2.	9,552	9,179	8,692	9,225	8,369
3.	8,898	8,340	7,204	2,110	9,489
4.	6,639	4,992	2,535	9,209	5,608
5.	9,993	9,285	6,596	9,114	10,232

	a	b	c
6.	4,537	9,529	8,356
7.	8,322	8,981	5,223

Mixed Practice

	a	b
1.	9 ten thousands	5 hundred thousands

	a	b	c	d
2.	1,010	1,386	645	939

Answer Key

Page 11

1.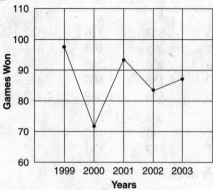

2.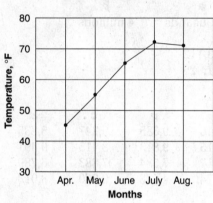

3.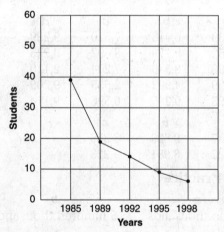

4.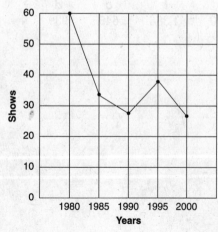

Page 12

1. three hundred sixty-four thousand, three hundred twenty-one
2. six hundred ninety-seven million, seven hundred sixty-two thousand
3. one million, three hundred seventy-five thousand
4. two thousand, five hundred ninety-one

5. 406,699
6. 920,100,000
7. 2,140
8. 1,000,320
9. 2,740 radio stations
10. 330 gallons

Page 13

	a	b	c	d	e
1.	662	1,350	781	771	1,880
2.	578	423	511	323	174
3.	1,089	1,266	1,342	1,619	1,700

	a	b
4.	1,433	756

Page 14

	a	b	c	d
1.	546	574	247	403
2.	709	309	359	103
3.	165	431	874	252
4.	89	99	422	469

Page 15

	a	b	c	d	e
1.	543	309	888	346	86
2.	187	388	767	191	280
3.	316	799	832	443	541
4.	691	706	312	78	154

	a	b	c
5.	277	439	419
6.	71	256	693

Mixed Practice

	a	b
1.	8 ten thousands	4 hundred thousands

	a	b	c
2.	946	1,304	1,590

Page 16

	a	b	c	d
1.	3,955	1,257	8,748	2,673
2.	767	395	3,947	2,873
3.	772	534	1,565	2,897
4.	2,096	4,280	7,244	1,472

Page 17

	a	b	c	d	e
1.	3,259	2,553	1,594	1,579	688
2.	3,490	6,145	8,518	3,883	1,357
3.	1,524	2,762	5,964	112	3,537
4.	2,569	324	883	5,455	4,892
5.	2,891	2,037	2,482	2,920	802

	a	b	c
6.	2,857	1,081	7,606
7.	2,094	7,763	945

Mixed Practice

1. three hundred sixty-eight thousand, nine hundred forty-seven
2. one million, seven hundred eight thousand, five hundred fifty-four

	a	b	c	d
3.	4,511	8,007	6,230	9,585

Page 18

	a	b	c	d
1.	100,114	103,013	158,441	70,042
2.	89,866	29,910	44,003	60,010
3.	20,008	94,976	19,000	19,000
4.	28,467	28,888	27,788	35,389
5.	18,989	18,849	26,425	49,997
6.	64,909	26,000	52,379	63,776

	a	b
7.	13,153	76,000

Page 19

	a	b	c	d
1.	20,768	89,673	63,596	105,712
2.	116,844	8,285	46,724	4,096
3.	57,383	70,609	8,914	86,893
4.	16,996	82,762	45,179	1,973

	a	b
5.	19,338	93,943
6.	13,501	41,626

Mixed Practice

	a	b	c	d
1.	25	6	42	6
2.	5	27	8	32

Page 20

	a	b	c	d
1.	600	700	600	500
2.	900	900	700	700
3.	800	900	800	900

	a	b	c	d
4.	100	500	400	400
5.	600	300	600	900

Page 21

	a	b	c	d
1.	600	600	700	900
2.	300	500	500	1,000
3.	1,100	6,800	4,600	4,400
4.	3,700	9,100	7,000	6,900
5.	6,000	8,000	1,000	9,000

Mixed Practice

	a	b	c	d
1.	878	631	217	644

	a	b	c
2.	26,487	1,268,047	34,587
3.	66,859,105	3,001,247	9,985,726
4.	1,123,647	254,987	104,875

Page 23

1. $69
2. $112
3. 45 acres of corn
4. 4:30
5. 20 hamsters
6. $56

Page 24

1. 787 feet
2. 412 Nobel prizes
3. 4,250,000 miles
4. 4,189 times
5. 83,861 square miles
6. 8,354 feet
7. about 400 miles
8. about 700 species

Page 25   Unit 1 Review

	a	b
1.	hundred thousands	thousands
2.	millions	ten thousands
3.	tens	hundreds
4.	ten millions	ones
5.	hundred thousands	tens

	a	b
6.	0 hundreds	3 ones
7.	9 hundred thousands	5 tens
8.	6 thousands	1 hundred million
9.	7 millions	2 ones
10.	6 thousands	8 ten thousands

11. 72,085
12. 2,040,506
13. 17,500,018
14. 322,069
15. 58,402

16. twenty-one thousand, one hundred six
17. four hundred three thousand, eight hundred seventy-two
18. one million, seven hundred twenty thousand, five hundred sixty-four
19. twenty-six thousand, eight hundred thirty-nine
20. thirty-five million, eighty-five thousand, three hundred forty

Answer Key

Page 26   Unit 1 Review

	a	b	c	d
21.	657	259	1,709	965
22.	1,170	42,570	100,121	30,004

	a	b
23.	1,392	15,216

	a	b	c	d
24.	287	790	375	398
25.	24,989	29,988	15,380	50,050

	a	b
26.	137	8,756

	a	b	c	d
27.	700	800	400	600
28.	1,500	800	5,300	400

Page 27   Unit 1 Review

29.

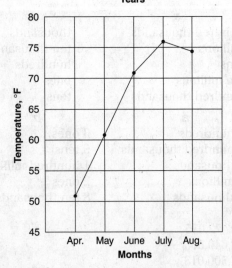

30.

31. 53 cars   32. $100

UNIT 2
Page 28

	a	b	c	d	e
1.	224	135	174	448	294
2.	688	594	222	224	672

	a	b	c	d
3.	2,217	1,855	3,879	2,865
4.	1,350	1,638	3,264	3,069

Page 29

	a	b	c	d	e
1.	445	1,248	684	692	1,628
2.	1,744	216	4,266	1,587	576
3.	2,262	1,379	2,088	2,184	2,330
4.	498	2,241	1,276	1,782	2,304

	a	b	c
5.	166	455	1,477
6.	462	360	2,871

Mixed Practice

	a	b	c	d
1.	32,721	74,343	6,656	2,908

Page 30

	a	b	c	d
1.	182	902	1,458	2,144
2.	420	1,218	2,730	6,132
3.	1,014	969	5,103	5,060

Page 31

	a	b	c	d	e
1.	1,995	1,200	4,085	828	2,968
2.	1,260	7,296	276	1,596	1,513
3.	432	1,364	936	7,623	2,016

	a	b	c
4.	1,716	4,089	4,148
5.	476	2,516	588

Mixed Practice

	a	b	c	d	e
1.	85	450	45	144	145
2.	289	1,074	682	472	332

Page 32

	a	b	c	d
1.	18,525	17,328	4,582	3,616
2.	11,040	5,376	17,408	19,872
3.	8,567	44,631	48,790	18,117

	a	b	c
4.	27,512	45,738	20,832

Page 33

	a	b	c	d	e
1.	90	120	70	240	240
2.	58,138	14,896	12,180	9,996	22,311
3.	1,250	650	3,850	960	420
4.	10,140	32,240	23,400	18,360	2,000

Page 35

1. 302 calories	2. $30
3. 25 miles	4. 700 pounds
5. 365 miles	6. 24 hours

Answer Key

Page 36
1. 11,350 grams
2. 6,436 meters
3. $12,520
4. 3,380 miles
5. $600
6. 144 grams
7. 665 pounds
8. 1,400 miles

Page 37

	a	b	c	d
1.	1,800	600	500	1,400
2.	2,100	5,600	2,400	800
3.	2,700	3,200	3,000	4,500
4.	3,600	1,600	2,000	1,600

	a	b	c
5.	1,800	900	1,500

Page 38

	a	b	c	d
1.	51,728	109,000	135,903	664,686
2.	53,824	233,280	263,466	493,020

Page 39

	a	b	c	d
1.	69,799	582,294	59,488	340,308
2.	45,850	151,848	423,540	241,240
3.	81,880	158,630	343,140	189,732

	a	b	c
4.	94,185	233,760	266,868

Mixed Practice

	a	b	c	d
1.	421	625	1,218	323
2.	42,054	3,021	28,512	1,270

Page 40

	a	b	c	d
1.	47,376	18,748	17,276	40,000
2.	46,908	75,475	162,699	630,000
3.	129,168	270,000	854,464	798,000

	a	b	c
4.	9,306	347,769	72,898

Page 41

	a	b	c	d
1.	17,990	24,828	17,130	27,000
2.	29,712	139,032	241,985	560,000
3.	171,798	150,000	72,618	448,575
4.	912,656	413,976	2,400,000	3,052,133

	a	b	c
5.	16,434	58,264	94,525

Mixed Practice

	a	b	c	d
1.	100	1,400	3,000	8,600

Page 43
1. 350 miles
2. 57,099 tons
3. 10,000 sweat glands
4. 165,000 miles
5. 10,000 pounds
6. 456,000 feet

Page 44
1. 1,825 times
2. about 600 miles
3. about 800,000 sq. mi
4. 160,500 people
5. $32,136
6. 282 ounces
7. 432 months
8. 17,776 kilometers

Page 45   Unit 2 Review

	a	b	c	d
1.	145	540	468	2,170
2.	1,472	2,006	765	28,612
3.	23,976	6,110	40,368	10,850
4.	445	3,744	4,108	19,786

	a	b	c
5.	4,404	1,836	1,860
6.	1,168	975	960
7.	18,538	11,319	9,240

Page 46   Unit 2 Review

	a	b	c	d
8.	420	360	280	270
9.	140,000	384,290	73,710	174,636
10.	10,420	176,076	174,435	497,574

	a	b	c
11.	386,862	66,043	124,800
12.	138,504	86,964	48,060

	a	b	c	d
13.	1,200	3,600	1,200	2,000
14.	1,200	900	4,200	4,000

Page 47   Unit 2 Review
15. 12 miles
16. 185 hours
17. 7,540 people
18. about 34,500 times
19. 725 feet
20. 5,100 gallons

UNIT 3

Page 48

	a	b	c	d	e
1.	12	19	27	473	121
2.	98	56	22	93	141

Page 49

	a	b	c
1.	48	28	16
2.	73	87	39
3.	79	84	94

	a	b	c
4.	16	87	99
5.	25	92	87

Answer Key

Mixed Practice

	a	b	c	d	e
1.	3,224	5,285	2,950	3,276	3,811

Page 50

	a	b	c	d
1.	11 R1	14 R2	15 R1	12 R4
2.	1 R2	34 R3	863 R7	144 R5

Page 51

	a	b	c	d
1.	9 R5	13 R3	28 R1	33 R2
2.	86 R3	58 R1	42 R6	61 R8
3.	149 R3	119 R6	296 R2	119 R5
4.	421 R1	212 R4	361 R3	374 R5

	a	b	c
5.	18 R1	13 R2	23 R7
6.	57 R3	125 R2	23 R4

Page 52

	a	b	c	d
1.	109 R4	407 R1	105 R3	307 R2
2.	50	40 R2	803 R7	604

Page 53

	a	b	c	d
1.	18 R37	32 R18	43	22 R5
2.	13	37 R30	26	49 R20

	a	b	c
3.	64 R5	27 R50	47

Page 55

1. division; 24 hours
2. subtraction; 511 free throws
3. subtraction; 57 years
4. multiplication; 8,250 pounds
5. division; 16 words
6. multiplication; 84,800 miles

Page 56

1.	$61		2.	217 yards
3.	13 nickels		4.	44 hours
5.	171 sequins; 1 left over		6.	5 cookies
7.	710 pounds		8.	22 points

Page 57

	a	b	c
1.	90	60	40
2.	80	50	40

	a	b	c
3.	20	30	30
4.	20	30	20

Page 58

	a	b
1.	too large; 3	too small; 3
2.	too large; 2	too large; 6
3.	too small; 8	too large; 4

Page 59

	a	b
1.	too large; 1	too small; 8
2.	too large; 1	too small; 7
3.	too large; 5	too large; 3
4.	too small; 7	too small; 8
5.	too large; 3	too small; 6

Mixed Practice

	a	b
1.	6 thousands	6 tens
2.	6 hundreds	2 ten thousands
3.	4 hundred thousands	6 millions
4.	40,230	
5.	708,005	
6.	11,010,500	
7.	65,984	

Page 60

	a	b	c
1.	14 R27	22	15 R39
2.	9 R60	2 R22	4 R18
3.	324 R5	418 R7	675 R8

Page 61

	a	b	c	d
1.	7 R4	5	6	3 R3
2.	31	21	20 R19	39 R8
3.	16	51 R7	73	304 R8
4.	314	524 R15	409 R47	168

	a	b	c
5.	3 R2	21	13 R8

Mixed Practice

	a	b	c	d
1.	439	4,898	238 R3	17,056

Page 63

1.	2,169 people		2.	528 feet
3.	8 days		4.	6,815 feet
5.	4,200 times		6.	15 hours

Page 64

1.	110 calories		2.	21 miles per gallon
3.	409 performances		4.	about 12 times
5.	65 pounds		6.	$19 an hour
7.	139 pounds		8.	16 dozen

Answer Key

Page 65　Unit 3 Review

	a	b	c	d
1.	23	75	59	12
2.	16 R2	93 R3	60 R5	507
3.	214 R4	921 R1	304 R7	1,524 R1
4.	42	35	90 R50	20 R8

	a	b	c
5.	21	139	46
6.	6 R4	15 R3	34 R1
7.	48 R25	44 R20	53 R40

Page 66　Unit 3 Review

	a	b	c
8.	60	30	40
9.	10	20	30

	a	b
10.	correct; 7	too large; 7
11.	too small; 8	too large; 3

	a	b	c	d
12.	26	21	38 R4	64 R25

	a	b	c
13.	5	20 R29	17 R24

Page 67　Unit 3 Review

14. multiplication; 2,000 pounds　　15. division; 25 feet
16. 166 square miles　　17. 630 calories
18. 335 steps　　19. 393 kilometers

UNIT 4

Page 68

	a	b	c
1.	$\frac{1}{5}$ or one fifth	$\frac{3}{8}$ or three eighths	$\frac{1}{6}$ or one sixth
2.	$\frac{5}{9}$ or five ninths	$\frac{2}{6}$ or two sixths	$\frac{4}{5}$ or four fifths

	a	b	c
3.	$\frac{2}{7}$	$\frac{3}{4}$	$\frac{6}{9}$

	a	b	c
4.	five eighths	four sevenths	one fourth

Page 69

	a	b	c
1.	$\frac{1}{6}$ or one sixth	$\frac{6}{8}$ or six eighths	$\frac{3}{4}$ or three fourths

	a	b	c
2.	$\frac{9}{10}$	$\frac{6}{6}$	$\frac{2}{8}$
3.	$\frac{5}{7}$	$\frac{10}{12}$	$\frac{4}{9}$

	a	b	c
4.	one third	seven ninths	five fifths
5.	six sevenths	three tenths	nine twelfths

	a	b	c
6.	$\frac{4}{7}$ four sevenths	$\frac{5}{7}$ five sevenths	$\frac{2}{7}$ two sevenths

	a	b	c
7.	$\frac{6}{20}$ six twentieths	$\frac{11}{20}$ eleven twentieths	$\frac{8}{20}$ eight twentieths

Mixed Practice

	a	b	c
1.	54	24	33
2.	1,458	23 R10	8,307

Page 70

1. 2
2. 4
3. 6
4. 4

	a	b
5.	$\frac{3}{4} = \frac{6}{8}$	$\frac{1}{3} = \frac{2}{6}$
6.	$\frac{2}{3} = \frac{4}{6}$	$\frac{4}{5} = \frac{8}{10}$

Page 71

	a	b	c	d
1.	>	=	<	=
2.	<	>	>	<
3.	<	=	<	<
4.	=	>	=	<

	a			b		
5.	$\frac{3}{8}$	$\frac{3}{4}$	$\frac{7}{8}$	$\frac{1}{6}$	$\frac{1}{3}$	$\frac{3}{6}$
6.	$\frac{2}{6}$	$\frac{2}{3}$	$\frac{5}{6}$	$\frac{1}{4}$	$\frac{3}{3}$	$\frac{2}{4}$
7.	$\frac{1}{8}$	$\frac{3}{8}$	$\frac{3}{4}$	$\frac{1}{3}$	$\frac{3}{6}$	$\frac{2}{3}$
8.	$\frac{1}{6}$	$\frac{2}{6}$	$\frac{2}{3}$	$\frac{1}{4}$	$\frac{4}{8}$	$\frac{7}{8}$

Page 72

	a	b	c
1.	$\frac{4}{4}$, 4	$\frac{3}{3}$, 6	$\frac{4}{4}$, 12
2.	$\frac{2}{2}$, 6	$\frac{3}{3}$, 6	$\frac{8}{8}$, 8
3.	$\frac{3}{3}$, 9	$\frac{2}{2}$, 10	$\frac{2}{2}$, 4
4.	$\frac{4}{4}$, 8	$\frac{2}{2}$, 4	$\frac{5}{5}$, 15

	a	b	c	d
5.	8	3	14	4
6.	5	10	9	12
7.	6	15	6	14
8.	5	10	4	8
9.	5	10	4	3
10.	8	6	15	5

Answer Key

Page 73

	a	b	c
1.	$\frac{5}{5}, \frac{1}{3}$	$\frac{2}{2}, \frac{4}{5}$	$\frac{3}{3}, \frac{3}{4}$
2.	$\frac{2}{2}, \frac{2}{3}$	$\frac{2}{2}, \frac{7}{8}$	$\frac{5}{5}, \frac{2}{5}$
3.	$\frac{2}{2}, \frac{1}{4}$	$\frac{4}{4}, \frac{1}{2}$	$\frac{3}{3}, \frac{1}{3}$
4.	$\frac{8}{8}, \frac{1}{2}$	$\frac{2}{2}, \frac{1}{8}$	$\frac{2}{2}, \frac{1}{2}$

	a	b	c	d
5.	$\frac{3}{4}$	$\frac{1}{3}$	$\frac{1}{3}$	$\frac{2}{3}$
6.	$\frac{1}{4}$	$\frac{3}{5}$	$\frac{2}{3}$	$\frac{1}{5}$
7.	$\frac{1}{6}$	$\frac{1}{5}$	$\frac{1}{2}$	$\frac{2}{3}$
8.	$\frac{4}{7}$	$\frac{1}{5}$	$\frac{5}{9}$	$\frac{3}{4}$
9.	$\frac{5}{6}$	$\frac{1}{4}$	$\frac{2}{7}$	$\frac{4}{5}$
10.	$\frac{1}{2}$	$\frac{4}{9}$	$\frac{2}{5}$	$\frac{3}{8}$

Page 74

	a	b	c	d
1.	4	2	6	7
2.	7	3	14	1
3.	$1\frac{1}{12}$	$2\frac{4}{7}$	$3\frac{1}{4}$	$3\frac{2}{5}$
4.	$1\frac{7}{8}$	$1\frac{1}{11}$	$1\frac{7}{9}$	$2\frac{2}{3}$
5.	$\frac{9}{5}$	$\frac{31}{7}$	$\frac{10}{9}$	$\frac{15}{4}$
6.	$\frac{21}{4}$	$\frac{12}{5}$	$\frac{27}{8}$	$\frac{13}{8}$

Page 75

	a	b	c	d
1.	$1\frac{1}{5}$	$1\frac{2}{3}$	$5\frac{1}{3}$	$1\frac{1}{2}$
2.	$2\frac{2}{5}$	$5\frac{1}{3}$	$1\frac{1}{3}$	$4\frac{3}{4}$
3.	$1\frac{3}{4}$	$3\frac{5}{6}$	$6\frac{1}{2}$	$2\frac{1}{2}$
4.	4	1	2	9
5.	$\frac{17}{4}$	$\frac{11}{3}$	$\frac{9}{2}$	$\frac{7}{6}$
6.	$\frac{9}{4}$	$\frac{15}{8}$	$\frac{13}{3}$	$\frac{19}{5}$
7.	$\frac{14}{3}$	$\frac{11}{10}$	$\frac{13}{5}$	$\frac{19}{7}$
8.	$\frac{20}{9}$	$\frac{22}{5}$	$\frac{11}{2}$	$\frac{25}{6}$

Mixed Practice

	a	b	c	d
1.	820	1,063	784	1,634
2.	5,491	5,015	1,703	273
3.	39,211	11,401	21,173	5,654

Page 76

	a	b	c	d	e
1.	$\frac{2}{3}$	$\frac{2}{3}$	$\frac{4}{7}$	$\frac{1}{2}$	$\frac{7}{9}$
2.	$1\frac{1}{5}$	$1\frac{2}{5}$	$1\frac{1}{8}$	$1\frac{1}{3}$	1
3.	$\frac{1}{2}$	$\frac{1}{3}$	$\frac{1}{4}$	$\frac{1}{2}$	$\frac{1}{3}$

Page 77

	a	b	c	d	e	f
1.	$\frac{3}{4}$	$\frac{5}{6}$	$\frac{5}{8}$	$\frac{4}{9}$	$\frac{5}{8}$	$\frac{5}{6}$
2.	$\frac{1}{2}$	$\frac{1}{4}$	$\frac{1}{2}$	$\frac{1}{3}$	$\frac{1}{3}$	$\frac{2}{3}$
3.	$\frac{5}{6}$	$\frac{7}{9}$	$\frac{1}{3}$	$\frac{3}{5}$	$\frac{1}{5}$	$\frac{3}{4}$
4.	$\frac{2}{5}$	$\frac{1}{5}$	$\frac{1}{5}$	$\frac{3}{4}$	$\frac{2}{3}$	$\frac{1}{2}$

	a	b	c
5.	$\frac{3}{4}$	$\frac{1}{4}$	$1\frac{1}{2}$

Mixed Practice

	a	b	c
1.	3,625,789	639,851	128,756,394

	a	b	c	d
2.	2,000	2,100	1,800	600

Page 78

	a	b	c	d	e
1.	$5\frac{1}{2}$	$9\frac{3}{4}$	$14\frac{4}{5}$	$9\frac{1}{2}$	$9\frac{3}{5}$
2.	$17\frac{4}{5}$	$15\frac{3}{4}$	$11\frac{2}{3}$	$21\frac{3}{5}$	$16\frac{2}{3}$
3.	$2\frac{5}{6}$	$1\frac{1}{2}$	$4\frac{1}{6}$	$2\frac{1}{5}$	$5\frac{2}{3}$
4.	$3\frac{1}{4}$	$5\frac{1}{4}$	$5\frac{2}{5}$	$1\frac{1}{3}$	$4\frac{2}{5}$

Page 79

	a	b	c	d	e
1.	$4\frac{2}{3}$	$5\frac{2}{5}$	$6\frac{1}{2}$	$10\frac{3}{8}$	$9\frac{5}{8}$
2.	$4\frac{3}{5}$	$6\frac{1}{2}$	$14\frac{3}{10}$	$19\frac{2}{5}$	$7\frac{5}{12}$
3.	$4\frac{1}{4}$	$1\frac{2}{5}$	$4\frac{1}{6}$	$3\frac{1}{2}$	$2\frac{3}{4}$
4.	$3\frac{1}{4}$	$4\frac{1}{8}$	$1\frac{2}{5}$	$2\frac{1}{2}$	$5\frac{2}{5}$

	a	b	c
5.	9	$2\frac{1}{2}$	$9\frac{5}{6}$
6.	$1\frac{1}{3}$	$9\frac{2}{3}$	$2\frac{2}{5}$

Page 81

1. Africa: $\frac{1}{5}$; Asia: $\frac{5}{9}$; North America: $\frac{1}{6}$

2. Kitti's hognosed bat: $\frac{7}{10}$ ounce; proboscis bat: $\frac{11}{10}$ ounce; banana bat: $\frac{9}{10}$ ounce

3. New York: $\frac{7}{10}$; Cleveland: $\frac{1}{2}$; Boston: $\frac{5}{9}$

4. petroleum: $\frac{2}{5}$; natural gas: $\frac{1}{4}$; coal: $\frac{1}{5}$

Page 82

1. 1 foot   2. 1 pound
3. $\frac{3}{4}$ dollar   4. $\frac{3}{4}$ lb
5. $\frac{1}{10}$ more blonds   6. $\frac{7}{25}$ more people
7. $\frac{7}{10}$ water   8. 2,600 species

Answer Key

Page 83

	a	b
1.	about $\frac{1}{2}$	about 1
2.	about 0	about 0
3.	about 1	about $\frac{1}{2}$

	a	b	c
4.	1	1	1
5.	0	1	$\frac{1}{2}$
6.	1	$\frac{1}{2}$	1

Page 84

	a	b	c	d
1.	1; 2; $\frac{1}{2}$	3; 5; $\frac{4}{5}$	1; 6; $\frac{7}{8}$	3; 1; $\frac{2}{3}$
2.	6; 7; $1\frac{3}{10}$	12; 5; $1\frac{3}{14}$	8; 6; $1\frac{5}{9}$	10; 9; $1\frac{7}{12}$
3.	5; 8; $1\frac{1}{12}$	3; 6; $1\frac{1}{8}$	8; 8; 1	3; 7; $1\frac{1}{9}$

Page 85

	a	b	c	d
1.	$\frac{3}{8}$	$\frac{1}{2}$	$\frac{4}{5}$	$\frac{7}{8}$
2.	$1\frac{1}{10}$	$\frac{11}{12}$	$1\frac{1}{9}$	$1\frac{5}{12}$
3.	$1\frac{3}{8}$	$1\frac{5}{9}$	$1\frac{1}{8}$	$1\frac{7}{10}$
4.	$\frac{5}{6}$	$1\frac{2}{9}$	$\frac{5}{9}$	$1\frac{1}{10}$

	a	b	c
5.	$1\frac{1}{12}$	$\frac{13}{16}$	$\frac{15}{16}$
6.	$1\frac{5}{8}$	$1\frac{3}{14}$	$1\frac{3}{8}$

Mixed Practice

	a	b	c
1.	761	372	1,317

Page 86

	a	b	c	d
1.	4; 1; $\frac{3}{8}$	2; 1; $\frac{1}{6}$	3; 2; $\frac{1}{4}$	5; 4; $\frac{1}{6}$
2.	13; 6; $\frac{1}{2}$	3; 1; $\frac{1}{3}$	8; 3; $\frac{1}{2}$	7; 5; $\frac{1}{10}$
3.	8; 1; $\frac{7}{10}$	13; 3; $\frac{2}{3}$	12; 1; $\frac{11}{16}$	11; 2; $\frac{3}{4}$

Page 87

	a	b	c	d
1.	$\frac{1}{8}$	$\frac{1}{10}$	$\frac{3}{8}$	$\frac{1}{8}$
2.	$\frac{1}{2}$	$\frac{1}{3}$	$\frac{1}{5}$	$\frac{5}{16}$
3.	$\frac{1}{9}$	$\frac{9}{16}$	$\frac{5}{9}$	$\frac{3}{10}$

	a	b	c
4.	$\frac{7}{20}$	$\frac{8}{15}$	$\frac{3}{16}$
5.	$\frac{1}{15}$	$\frac{1}{12}$	$\frac{2}{3}$

Mixed Practice

	a	b	c	d
1.	2,173	19,467	10,327	1,653
2.	46,922	14 R13	1,767 R11	10,381

Page 88

	a	b	c	d
1.	$9\frac{7}{8}$	4; $10\frac{5}{6}$	6; $5\frac{11}{12}$	2; $8\frac{7}{8}$
2.	$9\frac{2}{5}$	$14\frac{1}{2}$	$13\frac{5}{6}$	$7\frac{5}{6}$
3.	$16\frac{7}{8}$	$20\frac{7}{8}$	$11\frac{7}{9}$	$13\frac{7}{10}$
4.	$9\frac{7}{8}$	$23\frac{3}{4}$	$16\frac{1}{2}$	$17\frac{8}{9}$

Page 89

	a	b	c	d
1.	$10\frac{3}{5}$	$10\frac{7}{10}$	$9\frac{7}{8}$	$14\frac{1}{2}$
2.	$7\frac{11}{12}$	$5\frac{5}{8}$	$15\frac{2}{3}$	$27\frac{15}{16}$
3.	$37\frac{19}{20}$	$28\frac{7}{8}$	$53\frac{4}{5}$	$23\frac{2}{3}$
4.	$37\frac{9}{10}$	$33\frac{2}{3}$	$37\frac{11}{16}$	$42\frac{7}{8}$

	a	b	c
5.	$12\frac{3}{4}$	$31\frac{7}{9}$	$24\frac{1}{3}$
6.	$19\frac{4}{5}$	$38\frac{1}{4}$	$25\frac{11}{15}$

Mixed Practice

	a	b	c	d
1.	5,090	1,592	12,790	5,605

Page 90

	a	b	c	d
1.	$4\frac{2}{3}$	$7\frac{3}{10}$	$10\frac{1}{8}$	$13\frac{3}{4}$
2.	$5\frac{1}{3}$	$9\frac{1}{3}$	$8\frac{1}{2}$	$11\frac{3}{4}$

	a	b	c
3.	$4\frac{1}{4}$	$7\frac{3}{8}$	$9\frac{3}{10}$
4.	$13\frac{1}{4}$	$7\frac{1}{2}$	$9\frac{1}{6}$

Page 91

	a	b	c	d
1.	$7\frac{1}{4}$	$13\frac{7}{12}$	$13\frac{1}{20}$	$7\frac{1}{4}$
2.	$6\frac{3}{10}$	$9\frac{1}{9}$	$14\frac{3}{16}$	$12\frac{1}{8}$
3.	$12\frac{1}{6}$	$10\frac{1}{10}$	$11\frac{1}{5}$	$12\frac{1}{9}$
4.	$11\frac{1}{4}$	$21\frac{1}{8}$	$37\frac{1}{6}$	$10\frac{4}{9}$

	a	b	c
5.	$9\frac{3}{8}$	$12\frac{1}{2}$	$12\frac{1}{7}$
6.	$18\frac{1}{5}$	$15\frac{1}{14}$	$12\frac{2}{9}$

Mixed Practice

	a	b	c	d
1.	7,047	12,065	419	511 R30

Page 92

	a	b	c	d
1.	2; $6\frac{1}{2}$	2; $2\frac{1}{4}$	2; $6\frac{3}{8}$	5; $7\frac{1}{5}$
2.	$7\frac{3}{8}$	$6\frac{1}{3}$	$3\frac{1}{6}$	$5\frac{3}{8}$
3.	$7\frac{3}{8}$	$2\frac{5}{8}$	$6\frac{1}{2}$	$2\frac{5}{8}$
4.	$2\frac{1}{9}$	$3\frac{11}{14}$	$1\frac{1}{6}$	$3\frac{1}{6}$

Answer Key

Page 93

	a	b	c	d
1.	$2\frac{3}{10}$	$5\frac{1}{2}$	$8\frac{5}{8}$	$6\frac{7}{10}$
2.	$3\frac{3}{8}$	$8\frac{1}{2}$	$4\frac{3}{10}$	$2\frac{1}{8}$
3.	$8\frac{1}{4}$	$5\frac{9}{16}$	$1\frac{8}{15}$	$6\frac{2}{3}$
4.	$7\frac{9}{20}$	$9\frac{11}{16}$	$8\frac{5}{12}$	$8\frac{1}{9}$

	a	b	c
5.	$7\frac{3}{8}$	$6\frac{1}{3}$	$7\frac{1}{5}$
6.	$4\frac{3}{8}$	$4\frac{3}{10}$	$7\frac{7}{16}$

Mixed Practice

	a	b	c	d
1.	4,860	302	662	6,474

Page 94

	a	b	c	d
1.	$6; 3\frac{6}{6}$	$8; 5\frac{8}{8}$	$3; 1\frac{3}{3}$	$4; 6\frac{4}{4}$
2.	$5; 9\frac{5}{5}$	$3; 13\frac{3}{3}$	$6; 8\frac{6}{6}$	$4; 23\frac{4}{4}$

	a	b	c	d
3.	$4; 6\frac{1}{4}$	$3; 6\frac{2}{3}$	$4; 5\frac{3}{4}$	$8; 6\frac{5}{8}$
4.	$7\frac{5}{8}$	$16\frac{3}{10}$	$11\frac{13}{15}$	$6\frac{4}{9}$
5.	$11\frac{3}{8}$	$4\frac{5}{6}$	$12\frac{5}{9}$	$8\frac{4}{7}$

Page 95

	a	b	c	d
1.	$8\frac{4}{7}$	$4\frac{1}{6}$	$7\frac{1}{8}$	$8\frac{1}{2}$
2.	$5\frac{2}{5}$	$17\frac{3}{10}$	$9\frac{5}{12}$	$5\frac{3}{8}$
3.	$15\frac{1}{3}$	$19\frac{1}{8}$	$5\frac{1}{2}$	$18\frac{1}{4}$

	a	b	c
4.	$11\frac{5}{8}$	$11\frac{5}{9}$	$1\frac{5}{8}$
5.	$6\frac{11}{15}$	$16\frac{13}{16}$	$8\frac{7}{10}$

Mixed Practice

	a	b	c	d
1.	1,000	300	1,000	4,000

	a	b	c
2.	8,000	18,000	1,800

Page 96

	a	b	c
1.	$5\frac{4}{3}$	$7\frac{15}{8}$	$8\frac{7}{6}$
2.	$2\frac{14}{8}$	$4\frac{21}{12}$	$13\frac{18}{10}$

	a	b	c
3.	$4\frac{5}{8}$	$4\frac{1}{2}$	$6\frac{9}{10}$
4.	$1\frac{9}{10}$	$6\frac{5}{8}$	$4\frac{3}{4}$
5.	$6\frac{7}{9}$	$10\frac{7}{10}$	$5\frac{5}{6}$

Page 97

	a	b	c
1.	$3\frac{7}{16}$	$4\frac{5}{8}$	$5\frac{5}{8}$
2.	$10\frac{8}{9}$	$20\frac{1}{4}$	$7\frac{15}{16}$
3.	$6\frac{5}{6}$	$10\frac{9}{16}$	$7\frac{5}{8}$

	a	b	c
4.	$6\frac{1}{2}$	$4\frac{5}{6}$	$5\frac{7}{8}$
5.	$15\frac{1}{2}$	$3\frac{11}{15}$	$7\frac{5}{6}$

Mixed Practice

	a	b	c	d
1.	312,416	67	44,180	1,251

Page 99

1. $\frac{11}{12}$ mile 2. $\frac{3}{4}$ cup
3. $\frac{5}{12}$ of the pizza 4. $\frac{9}{10}$ inch
5. $\frac{5}{8}$ inch 6. $\frac{7}{12}$ yard

Page 100

1. $15\frac{2}{3}$ miles 2. $7\frac{3}{4}$ pounds
3. $4\frac{1}{2}$ cups 4. $3\frac{1}{4}$ inches
5. $5\frac{11}{12}$ yards 6. $14\frac{1}{16}$ pounds
7. $4\frac{1}{2}$ inches 8. $3\frac{3}{5}$ ounces

Page 101 Unit 4 Review

	a	b	c	
1.	$\frac{3}{5}$	$\frac{4}{9}$	$\frac{1}{6}$	

	a		b	
2.	$\frac{1}{9}$ $\frac{3}{9}$ $\frac{2}{3}$		$\frac{3}{10}$ $\frac{3}{5}$ $\frac{4}{5}$	

	a	b	c	d
3.	$\frac{3}{4}$	$\frac{3}{5}$	$\frac{2}{3}$	$\frac{1}{2}$
4.	6	2	9	5

	a	b	c	d
5.	$\frac{7}{9}$	1	$\frac{5}{8}$	$\frac{3}{5}$
6.	$11\frac{3}{5}$	10	$7\frac{2}{3}$	$9\frac{2}{3}$
7.	$\frac{5}{8}$	$1\frac{1}{9}$	$\frac{9}{10}$	$\frac{9}{16}$
8.	$10\frac{7}{9}$	$11\frac{1}{6}$	$10\frac{7}{8}$	$7\frac{7}{15}$

Page 102 Unit 4 Review

	a	b	c	d
9.	$3\frac{7}{8}$	$2\frac{1}{6}$	5	$4\frac{3}{4}$
10.	$\frac{13}{3}$	$\frac{42}{5}$	$\frac{17}{8}$	$\frac{53}{10}$

	a	b	c	d
11.	2; $4\frac{2}{2}$	5; $7\frac{5}{5}$	9; $11\frac{9}{9}$	7; $15\frac{7}{7}$

	a	b	c	d
12.	$\frac{2}{5}$	$\frac{2}{7}$	$\frac{1}{3}$	$\frac{1}{2}$
13.	$5\frac{1}{3}$	$2\frac{2}{3}$	$4\frac{3}{5}$	$8\frac{3}{4}$
14.	$\frac{3}{8}$	$\frac{5}{9}$	$\frac{5}{16}$	$\frac{3}{5}$
15.	$5\frac{1}{2}$	$1\frac{3}{4}$	$3\frac{9}{10}$	$4\frac{5}{9}$

	a	b	c
16.	$\frac{1}{2}$	1	1

Page 103 Unit 4 Review

17. Atlanta: $\frac{2}{3}$; Philadelphia: $\frac{4}{9}$; New York: $\frac{5}{9}$

18. Goliath: $8\frac{3}{10}$ in.; Queen Alexandra: 11 in.; African swallowtail: $9\frac{1}{10}$ in.

19. $\frac{5}{12}$ mile   20. $\frac{5}{8}$ gallon

UNIT 5

Page 104

	a	b	c
1.	0.3	0.8	2.4
2.	0.32	0.68	1.21

	a	b	c
3.	$1.00	$0.10	$0.01
4.	$12.00	$0.30	$0.08

Page 105

	hundreds	tens	ones	tenths	hundredths	thousandths
1.		2	9	0	1	
2.			0	4	8	5
3.			3	7	8	2
4.		6	7	5	6	7
5.			1	0	0	
6.	1	4	2	0	4	

	a	b	c
7.	tenths	hundredths	thousandths
8.	thousandths	ones	thousandths
9.	hundredths	tens	tenths

	a	b	c
10.	3 thousandths	9 hundredths	4 thousandths
11.	5 hundredths	3 ones	8 hundredths
12.	4 ones	8 thousandths	6 ones

Page 106

	a	b	c
1.	hundredths	thousandths	tenths
2.	tenths	hundredths	thousandths
3.	tenths	thousandths	hundredths

	a	b
4.	0.4	0.04
5.	0.004	0.504
6.	0.016	0.16
7.	10.13	54.01

8. forty-eight thousandths
9. sixty-four hundredths
10. nine and four tenths
11. one hundred thirty and seventy hundredths
12. one and five hundred thirty-two thousandths

Page 107

	a	b
1.	0.5	0.89
2.	3.004	0.63
3.	4.7	8.05
4.	0.31	0.028
5.	2.03	0.14
6.	60.4	5.6
7.	0.017	8.009
8.	9.09	0.23
9.	70.1	0.71

10. twenty-three hundredths
11. eight tenths
12. four and fifty-three hundredths
13. six and nine thousandths
14. nine and eight hundred two thousandths
15. five and seventy-five thousandths
16. seven and five tenths
17. eighteen and four hundredths
18. eighteen hundredths

Mixed Practice

	a	b	c
1.	876	2,607	50,344
2.	24,218	471,230	168 R1

Page 108

	a	b	c
1.	<	<	>
2.	<	<	>
3.	=	>	<

	a			b		
4.	1.4	14.0	140	0.007	0.07	0.7
5.	3.45	34.5	345	0.79	0.80	0.81

Answer Key

Page 109

	a	b	c
1.	>	<	<
2.	<	<	=
3.	=	>	>
4.	>	>	<
5.	=	>	=
6.	<	>	<

	a			b		
7.	$1.70	$17.0	$170	0.06	0.066	0.60
8.	5.06	5.6	5.602	0.003	0.03	0.3
9.	1.2	2.1	21	0.007	0.090	0.8

Mixed Practice

	a	b	c	d
1.	$11\frac{2}{3}$	$9\frac{3}{4}$	$13\frac{1}{2}$	$7\frac{1}{4}$

	a	b	c
2.	$\frac{2}{3}$	$5\frac{5}{8}$	$7\frac{7}{8}$
3.	$3\frac{1}{2}$	$8\frac{3}{8}$	$4\frac{1}{8}$

Page 110

	a	b	c	d
1.	$\frac{3}{10}$	$\frac{7}{10}$	$\frac{9}{10}$	$\frac{1}{10}$
2.	$\frac{3}{100}$	$\frac{7}{100}$	$\frac{9}{100}$	$\frac{1}{100}$
3.	$2\frac{3}{10}$	$6\frac{9}{10}$	$3\frac{7}{10}$	$8\frac{1}{10}$
4.	$9\frac{88}{100}$	$5\frac{7}{100}$	$4\frac{90}{100}$	$2\frac{25}{100}$

	a	b	c	d
5.	0.4	0.8	0.6	0.2
6.	0.23	0.97	0.246	0.810
7.	5.1	2.7	3.8	9.4
8.	3.06	9.01	8.825	6.975

Page 111

	a	b	c
1.	0.75	0.2	0.96
2.	0.8	0.35	0.15
3.	0.24	0.5	0.52
4.	3.4	4.5	2.55
5.	2.72	8.25	6.8

	a	b
6.	4.15	20.2
7.	3.08	11.5
8.	7.45	5.88

Page 113

1. 18 inches
2. $2\frac{1}{4}$ pounds
3. Subtract $\frac{1}{10}$; $\frac{3}{5}$
4. Subtract 0.2; 8.12
5. Add 3; 13 toothpicks
6. Add 11; 66

Page 114

1. 1.5
2. 0.04
3. 16.94
4. 49.94

5. one hundred forty-seven dollars and thirty-eight cents
6. twenty-four and five hundred forty-seven thousandths
7. one sixteenth
8. thirty-eight cents

9. Washington, D.C.
10. Key West

Page 115

	a	b	c	d
1.	4	3	2	7
2.	32	41	34	63
3.	40	82	79	51
4.	7	2	3	9

	a	b	c	d
5.	$3.00	$14.00	$9.00	$5.00
6.	$9.00	$4.00	$1.00	$73.00
7.	$313.00	$8.00	$0	$40.00
8.	$1.00	$3.00	$10.00	$26.00

	a	b	c	d
9.	0.4	0.7	0.8	0.5
10.	6.3	9.1	4.6	7.4
11.	82.8	29.9	85.5	60.0
12.	80	57.7	60.6	30.5

Page 116

	a	b	c	d
1.	26.5	76.8	91.5	77.2
2.	8.813	5.882	9.991	64.190
3.	$2.25	$9.78	1.265	67.837
4.	10.15	9.59	15.69	$13.75

Page 117

	a	b	c	d	e
1.	5.9	7.2	76.4	17.1	83.6
2.	7.33	4.28	37.91	7.74	1.49
3.	$51.26	$9.74	$79.51	$84.70	$7.14
4.	0.906	10.245	9.272	51.507	74.264
5.	294.2	98.67	1.25	5.939	82.28

	a	b	c
6.	1.5	4.5	95.8
7.	$10.58	$8.99	$90.00
8.	8.988	14.197	4.405
9.	11.5	17.2	16.6
10.	7.05	44.47	67.835

Answer Key

Page 118

	a	b	c	d	e
1.	19.7	5.87	149.956	18.06	17.5
2.	15.1	25.88	9.08	15.001	10.207
3.	$30.80	$256.10	$125.14	1.806	4.258

	a	b
4.	10.1	$15.20
5.	20.8	22.983

Mixed Practice

	a	b	c	d	e
1.	8	43	17	31	10
2.	0.5	1.7	12.3	7.9	23.2

Page 119

	a	b	c	d
1.	9	$13	$109	$86
2.	17	119	8	39

	a	b	c	d
3.	1.2	6.8	17.3	$99.50
4.	53.1	1.2	4.7	6.6

Page 120

	a	b	c	d
1.	48.5	8.4	$43.71	$7.91
2.	1.88	4.31	10.94	32.28
3.	3.917	1.737	1.117	7.838
4.	8.363	2.236	1.226	4.505

Page 121

	a	b	c	d	e
1.	1.8	2.6	6.5	3.4	11.1
2.	5.29	0.58	10.89	5.22	0.38
3.	$3.64	$2.64	$4.18	$10.75	$12.30
4.	3.412	3.908	11.721	5.723	16.224

	a	b	c
5.	5.9	5.16	1.379
6.	1.71	7.796	4.775

Mixed Practice

	a	b	c	d	e
1.	$\frac{1}{5}$	1	$\frac{1}{2}$	$40\frac{1}{5}$	$8\frac{2}{7}$
2.	$2\frac{4}{9}$	$13\frac{5}{6}$	$13\frac{11}{16}$	$14\frac{1}{2}$	$17\frac{7}{8}$

Page 122

	a	b	c	d	e
1.	10.7	23.67	88.94	6.3	68.5
2.	2.964	11.62	36.25	414.6	99.63
3.	$2.47	$7.41	$16.49	$54.69	$152.36

	a	b	c
4.	4.5	1.89	2.421
5.	8.44	$5.01	$6.48

Mixed Practice

	a	b	c	d
1.	$\frac{2}{10}$ or $\frac{1}{5}$	$\frac{15}{100}$ or $\frac{3}{20}$	$\frac{78}{100}$ or $\frac{39}{50}$	$\frac{9}{100}$
2.	0.75	0.125	0.4	0.55

Page 123

	a	b	c	d
1.	3	$4	5	$15
2.	1	3	5	25

	a	b	c	d
3.	0.4	2.5	8.8	12.3
4.	7.7	0.8	53.7	1.6

Page 125

1. about $72.00
2. about 28 meters
3. about 22 tons
4. about 486 inches
5. about 30 years
6. about 110 yards

Page 126

1. 31.4 years
2. 9 miles
3. 9.527 miles per hour
4. 0.06 meters
5. 4,902.3 miles
6. $33.98
7. 400.98 kilograms
8. 3.6°F

Page 127   Unit 5 Review

	a	b	c
1.	hundredths	thousandths	tenths
2.	3 tenths	0 hundredths	9 thousandths

	a	b
3.	0.014	0.07

4. eight and fifty-two hundredths
5. twelve and twenty-three thousandths

	a	b	c
6.	<	>	<

	a	b
7.	0.32 0.42 0.53	0.033 0.303 0.33

	a	b	c	d
8.	0.7	0.82	0.4	14.5

	a	b	c
9.	2.7	12.8	8.35

	a	b	c	d
10.	$\frac{41}{100}$	$\frac{63}{1,000}$	$\frac{8}{10}$	$3\frac{17}{100}$

Answer Key

Page 128   Unit 5 Review

	a	b	c	d	
11.	0.4	0.8	0.9	1.0	

	a	b	c	d	
12.	15	7	20	$13	

	a	b	c	d	e
13.	12.5	7.56	88.295	13.2	9.01
14.	1.6	1.589	9.63	0.61	2.235
15.	$9.36	$39.98	$18.25	$85.87	$8.76

	a	b	c	d
16.	13	$5	94	7

	a	b	c	d
17.	1.6	32.4	3.3	39.9

Page 129   Unit 5 Review

18. $1\frac{1}{4}$ in. a week   19. 4.2 miles
20. about 0 meters   21. yes
22. about 248 years   23. about 28 years

UNIT 6

Page 130

	a	b
1.	in.	ft
2.	mi	ft

	a	b	c
3.	1	1	3
4.	1	36	5,280

	a	b	c
5.	84	45	15,840
6.	216	10,560	15

	a	b	c
7.	$3\frac{1}{2}$	2	4
8.	$2\frac{11}{12}$	$5\frac{2}{3}$	2

Page 131

	a	b
1.	lb	T
2.	oz	lb

	a	b	c
3.	1	1	16

	a	b	c
4.	80	4,000	32
5.	14,000	96	144

	a	b	c
6.	$1\frac{1}{2}$	3	$1\frac{1}{2}$
7.	$2\frac{1}{4}$	$5\frac{3}{4}$	$3\frac{1}{8}$

Page 132

	a	b
1.	c	c
2.	pt or qt	gal

	a	b	c
3.	1	1	1
4.	16	1	1

	a	b	c
5.	28	48	16
6.	32	100	800

	a	b	c
7.	$1\frac{1}{2}$	3	1
8.	$2\frac{1}{2}$	$1\frac{7}{8}$	$1\frac{3}{4}$

Page 133

	a	b
1.	=	>
2.	>	=
3.	>	>
4.	>	<
5.	<	>
6.	>	=

Page 134

	a	b
1.	km	m
2.	m	m
3.	km	km
4.	km	m

	a	b
5.	125 km	2.8 m
6.	30 m	5 km

	a	b	c
7.	7,000	3,000	57,000

	a	b	c
8.	2	6	10

Page 135

	a	b
1.	cm	cm or mm
2.	mm	cm
3.	m	mm

	a	b
4.	1 cm	100 m
5.	3 m	25 cm

	a	b	c
6.	50	1,200	6,000

	a	b	c
7.	2	5	8

Page 136

	a	b
1.	kg	g
2.	kg	kg

	a	b
3.	9 kg	1 g
4.	500 g	18 kg

	a	b	c
5.	9,000	7,000	13,000

	a	b	c
6.	4	2	15

Page 137

	a	b
1.	mL	L
2.	L	mL

	a	b
3.	5,000 L	4 L
4.	700 mL	180 mL

	a	b	c
5.	10,000	4,000	250,000

	a	b	c
6.	5	6	30

Page 138

	a	b	c
1.	>	>	<
2.	<	<	<
3.	>	<	<

	a	b	c
4.	1,000	0.01	0.01
5.	1,000	0.001	1,000
6.	0.01	0.001	0.001

	a	b	c
7.	>	<	<
8.	<	>	>

Page 139

	a	b
1.	=	>
2.	>	>
3.	=	=
4.	=	>
5.	>	<
6.	>	<

Page 141

1. Kendra: 8 years old; Tim: 4 years old
2. 2 dimes, 2 nickels, 1 penny
3. gray whale: 36 tons; Baird's whale: 12 tons
4. Vatican City: 0.5 square kilometers; Monaco: 1.8 square kilometers
5. 20 grams
6. man: 1 gallon; woman: $\frac{1}{2}$ gallon

Page 142

1.	400 cups	2.	141 feet
3.	25 pounds	4.	24,912 miles
5.	178 centimeters	6.	256 pounds
7.	Syracuse	8.	Mexico

Page 143   Unit 6 Review

	a	b
1.	ft	T
2.	lb	pt or qt
3.	gal	in.

	a	b	c
4.	16	16	36
5.	10,560	108	60
6.	6,000	96	2,000

	a	b	c
7.	2	3	6
8.	4	1	3
9.	$1\frac{1}{3}$	$\frac{1}{2}$	6

	a	b
10.	<	>
11.	<	<
12.	<	>

Page 144   Unit 6 Review

	a	b
13.	2 cm	1 kg
14.	15 kg	33 m
15.	200 mL	1 L
16.	15 L	25 mm

	a	b	c
17.	5,000	9,000	230
18.	17,000	3,500	64,000
19.	300	5,000	20,000

	a	b	c
20.	70	9	5
21.	170	22	3
22.	8	4	2.5

	a	b
23.	<	<
24.	>	>

Page 145   Unit 6 Review

25.	3 dimes, 2 nickels, 3 pennies	26.	Ron: 4 goldfish Caroline: 7 goldfish
27.	one box: 24 cards one box: 12 cards	28.	basketballs: 9 footballs: 15
29.	ostrich: 100 inches	30.	Glenn: 67 years old Voss: 37 years old

Answer Key

UNIT 7

Page 146

	a	b	c	d
1.	∠LMN	∠EFG	∠PQR	∠K

	a	b	c	d
2.	obtuse angle	acute angle	right angle	obtuse angle

Page 147

	a	b	c	d
1.	∠R	∠ABC	∠WXY	∠D

	a	b	c	d
2.	right angle	acute angle	obtuse angle	right angle

	a	b	c	d
3.	obtuse angle	right angle	acute angle	obtuse angle

Mixed Review

	a	b	c	d
1.	1,048	201	2,189	19,391
2.	4,512	164 R3	9,963	963 R2

Page 148

	a	b	c
1.	8 units	8 units	10 units
2.	12 units	10 units	12 units
3.	16 units	12 units	14 units

Page 149

	a	b
1.	12 feet	14 meters
2.	18 yards	32 inches
3.	40 inches	17.8 meters

Page 150

	a	b
1.	5 square units	4 square units
2.	8 square units	15 square units
3.	9 square units	6 square units

Page 151

	a	b
1.	16 sq. yards	3 sq. feet
2.	4 sq. centimeters	12 sq. inches
3.	40 sq. meters	144 sq. millimeters

Page 153

1. 20 yards   2. 143 sq. feet
3. 12 feet   4. 96 sq. feet
5. 1 acre   6. 370 meters

Page 154

1. 1,500 sq. meters   2. 60 yards
3. acute angle   4. right angle
5. $126\frac{2}{3}$ yards   6. 88 inches
7. $210.00   8. 300 tiles

Page 155   Unit 7 Review

	a	b	c	d
1.	∠EFG	∠LMN	∠ABC	∠P

	a	b	c	d
2.	right angle	acute angle	obtuse angle	obtuse angle

	a	b	c
3.	10 units	16 units	14 units

	a	b	c
4.	5 square units	15 square units	4 square units

Page 156   Unit 7 Review

5. 20 feet   6. 1,508 square meters
7. 20 miles   8. 16 square feet
9. $1,296.00   10. 138 yards

FINAL REVIEW

Page 157

	a	b
1.	ten thousands	hundreds

2. 416,712
3. 2,594,003

	a	b	c
4.	>	=	<

	a	b	c	d
5.	988	18,641	31,193	641,173

	a	b	c	d
6.	149	489	381	11,198

	a	b
7.	796	920

	a	b	c	d
8.	1,600	1,700	3,600	8,500

Page 158

	a	b	c	d
9.	207	2,130	10,456	104,692
10.	2,775	29,610	24,976	284,262

	a	b	c	d
11.	31 R2	39 R18	88 R1	2,281 R40
12.	77 R2	16 R17	109	318

	a	b
13.	13,224	547 R5

	a	b	c	d
14.	1,800	600	90	7 or 8

Page 159

	a	b	c
15.	$\frac{2}{3}$	$\frac{5}{8}$	$\frac{1}{9}$

	a	b	c
16.	9 tenths	4 hundredths	5 thousandths

	a	b	c
17.	<	<	>

	a	b	c	d
18.	$\frac{27}{50}$	$4\frac{1}{5}$	$\frac{1}{2}$	$2\frac{9}{50}$

	a	b	c	d
19.	0.2	0.75	3.5	1.7

	a	b	c	d
20.	$\frac{7}{11}$	$\frac{1}{2}$	$9\frac{5}{7}$	$15\frac{2}{3}$
21.	$\frac{1}{3}$	$\frac{2}{3}$	$5\frac{7}{10}$	$6\frac{9}{10}$
22.	14.58	13.019	9.603	$160.07
23.	5.57	44.22	19.36	$17.26

Page 160

	a	b	c
24.	144	80	9,000
25.	8,000	5,400	24

	a	b	c
26.	2	1	3
27.	3	$1\frac{1}{2}$	6

	a	b
28.	<	>
29.	>	>

	a	b	c	d
30.	acute angle	obtuse angle	acute angle	right angle

	a	b	c
31.	Perimeter: 10 in.	20 cm	22 ft
	Area: 6 sq. in.	25 sq. cm	28 sq. ft

PRETEST

Page 8

1.	C	8.	A
2.	D	9.	D
3.	B	10.	D
4.	A	11.	B
5.	D	12.	D
6.	B	13.	C
7.	C	14.	A

PRETEST

Page 9

15.	C	23.	C
16.	A	24.	B
17.	C	25.	A
18.	B	26.	D
19.	C	27.	A
20.	C	28.	C
21.	A	29.	D
22.	D	30.	D

PRETEST

Page 10

31.	C	38.	C
32.	B	39.	D
33.	D	40.	A
34.	C	41.	C
35.	B	42.	B
36.	B	43.	C
37.	D	44.	D

PRETEST

Page 11

45.	B	51.	C
46.	A	52.	B
47.	D	53.	A
48.	A	54.	A
49.	D	55.	C
50.	C		

UNIT 1 TEST

Page 14

1.	C	8.	D
2.	D	9.	A
3.	A	10.	C
4.	C	11.	C
5.	D	12.	A
6.	B	13.	B
7.	A	14.	C

UNIT 2 TEST

Page 16

1.	C	9.	D
2.	A	10.	A
3.	B	11.	D
4.	C	12.	B
5.	A	13.	D
6.	A	14.	C
7.	B	15.	D
8.	C	16.	A

Answer Key

UNIT 3 TEST

Page 18

1.	D	10.	A
2.	D	11.	C
3.	B	12.	D
4.	B	13.	D
5.	D	14.	C
6.	C	15.	A
7.	C	16.	A
8.	A	17.	A
9.	A	18.	B

UNIT 4 TEST

Page 20

1.	A	9.	A
2.	D	10.	D
3.	B	11.	C
4.	C	12.	B
5.	B	13.	B
6.	C	14.	B
7.	D	15.	A
8.	C	16.	C

UNIT 5 TEST

Page 22

1.	D	9.	A
2.	A	10.	A
3.	A	11.	C
4.	C	12.	D
5.	C	13.	A
6.	B	14.	C
7.	B	15.	C
8.	C		

UNIT 6 TEST

Page 24

1.	B	9.	B
2.	D	10.	A
3.	B	11.	C
4.	C	12.	A
5.	C	13.	B
6.	C	14.	A
7.	B	15.	A
8.	B	16.	A

UNIT 7 TEST

Page 26

1.	C	7.	D
2.	D	8.	C
3.	C	9.	B
4.	B	10.	C
5.	C		
6.	B		

MASTERY TEST

Page 27

1.	A	8.	D
2.	C	9.	B
3.	D	10.	D
4.	D	11.	C
5.	C	12.	A
6.	A	13.	B
7.	B	14.	C

MASTERY TEST

Page 28

15.	C	23.	D
16.	A	24.	B
17.	C	25.	D
18.	D	26.	B
19.	A	27.	D
20.	A	28.	B
21.	A	29.	D
22.	B	30.	A

MASTERY TEST

Page 29

31.	C	39.	D
32.	D	40.	B
33.	A	41.	B
34.	B	42.	A
35.	B	43.	A
36.	D	44.	D
37.	B	45.	D
38.	A		

MASTERY TEST

Page 30

46.	C	52.	B
47.	B	53.	C
48.	A	54.	D
49.	C	55.	C
50.	B	56.	B
51.	D	57.	C